A Life in History

A Life in History

JOHN DAVIES
TRANSLATED BY JON GOWER

First impression: 2015

© Copyright Janet Davies and Y Lolfa Cyf., 2015

The publishers wish to acknowledge the support of
Cyngor Llyfrau Cymru

Cover photograph: Emyr Young / Llenyddiaeth Cymru
Cover design: Y Lolfa

ISBN: 978 1 78461 217 7

Published and printed in Wales
on paper from well-maintained forests by
Y Lolfa Cyf., Talybont, Ceredigion SY24 5HE
website www.ylolfa.com
e-mail ylolfa@ylolfa.com
tel 01970 832 304
fax 832 782

Acknowledgements

THANKS TO JOHN'S family for supporting the idea of this translation, especially to Anna Brychan for her ready enthusiasm. The book benefited hugely from having Janet Davies's experienced eye cast over the proofs. Diolch yn fawr iawn am y mewnbwn hwnnw, Janet.

I should also like to thank Lefi Gruffudd at Y Lolfa for his unstinting support and to Eirian Jones, the English-language editor at the press, for her careful reading and detailed suggestions.

But my deepest thanks go to John himself, who gave so many of us the great gift of his company and wisdom. He helped teach a nation about itself and then went further, explaining Wales to the larger world and doing so with an infectious zeal and a boundless gusto.

John was a national treasure and a nation's historian at a necessary time. We miss him profoundly even as we begin to fully appreciate him and his towering contribution.

Jon Gower
November 2015

Contents

Contents

1

Treorci

1938–45

THE NEWS ON 25 April 1938 was depressing. It had been announced that Jews were no longer allowed to frequent the restaurants of Vienna, while Konrad Henlein declared that he hoped Hitler's army would arrive before too long to ensure an end to the alleged suffering of the Germans of the Sudetenland.

Two days later there was much better news. On 27 April a notice was placed on the front page of the *Western Mail* (a page that was reserved, in those days, simply for family and business advertisements) announcing that a son (John) had been born at Llwynypia Hospital to Mary (née Potter) and Daniel Davies of Dumfries Street, Treorci.

Later, I was given a description of the day of my birth. I heard how my Auntie Bet from Stuart Road, Treorci, lifted me so that I could see out through the window, granting me a view of the railway, the river, the main road and the rows of houses that threaded their way along the base of the hill on which the hospital stood. That was the iconic view of the Rhondda, a landscape which is a part of both my inheritance and mission to this day. Years later I wrote a volume about the hundred places in Wales one should see before dying. One of those was the landscape of the Rhondda, and I insisted that anyone who hadn't seen that view had not really seen Wales.

It is interesting to linger over the names Dumfries

Street and Stuart Street; the latter was one of a legion of Rhondda names associated with the Crichton Stuart family, Marquesses of Bute. (I was disappointed to learn that there wasn't a member of that family whose name was Cemetery – the name of the street which runs from the Cardiff Arms on Bute Street to the lower reaches of Orci Vale.)

As a boy I was intrigued by the connections with Scotland and when I was given the opportunity to work towards a doctorate, I plumped for the Marquesses of Bute and their activities in Glamorgan as my chosen subject.

But the street names were mere details when compared with the myriad pleasures I had at home in Dumfries Street. The member of my family I remember best is my sister Anne. Two years older, she was always, as the poet Waldo Williams puts it when describing the Preseli mountains, 'wrth fy nghefn yn mhob annibyniaeth barn' [at my back in all independent judgment]. My sister and I travelled together many times and I well remember our failed attempts to shuck oysters at a youth hostel in Morlaix by boiling them, and the joys of being in her company listening to the chimes of cattle bells in the south of Bavaria.

Of course, my parents were a dear and essential part of this story. Both of them had forebears who migrated to the Rhondda and I have heard a rumour that some of our ancestors had been living there before the coal mines were sunk, but I have found no evidence to confirm this. The later generations are the important ones, as they accounted for the fact that the population of Ystradyfodwg rose from fewer than a thousand people in 1840 to over one hundred and sixty thousand by the 1920s, when more people lived there than in Cardiganshire, Meirionethshire, Montgomeryshire and Radnorshire put together.

The census of 1861 notes that John Davies, my great-grandfather, was a lead miner who lived in Pontrhydfendigaid, in Cardiganshire. His son, William, was married in Llanbadarn Fawr in the early 1880s, when he was employed as a farm labourer in a place called Y Gors in the valley of the river Paith. His wife, Jane Richards, was a servant who lived in a cottage known as Bryn-bedd on Mynydd Bach. Jane was part of a large family, and, as a consequence, it has been a pleasure to encounter cousins the length and breadth of Glamorgan and Cardiganshire.

A son, John Davies, was born to Jane and William in 1882, a key figure both in Welsh history and in my own. As incomes in rural Cardiganshire in the 1880s were pitifully low, the obvious answer to their situation was to move to the Rhondda. There, two months after the birth of my father, Daniel Davies, in the Rhondda Fach in October 1885, his father, William, was killed in the Maerdy colliery disaster. I found his grave in Glyn-rhedyn cemetery – the first to be buried of eighty-one men who were killed underground that day. (I am sure William would have felt utterly hopeless about his family's fate as the flames lapped around him. I should be delighted if I could tell him that he had a granddaughter and a grandson, four great-grandchildren and six great-great-grandchildren, all living in quite comfortable circumstances.)

His wife's fate was recounted in copious correspondence between John, the elder of Jane's sons, and that influential man, Thomas Jones of Rhymney, a clerk at the ironworks who eventually became a professor of Economics, assistant secretary in David Lloyd George's cabinet, and one of the founders of Coleg Harlech. Jane Davies received five shillings a week with which to support herself, minus four pence, the cost of the postal order. This was a source of some bitterness to John, but his principal grievance was a stipulation that his mother was regularly required to obtain a magistrate's report that she remained 'of good character'. Her two sons received half a crown a week to be shared between them until they reached the age of thirteen, and the magistrate was required to testify that each was still alive to justify that payment. The family duly moved back to Cardiganshire, and set up home in a dilapidated earthen cottage in Llangeitho, where the sons had to climb up ropes to bed.

Their mother supplemented her income by working as a midwife and labouring in the fields. Later on, her sons secured her a terraced house in Meidrim Road and there she prepared meals for the pupils of Llangeitho Primary School, including E. D. Jones who would become the Librarian at the National Library in Aberystwyth. In the 1980s, Mari James, Llangeitho, introduced me to a neighbour of hers. 'This one,' she said, 'is Jane Maerdy's grandson' – even though Jane had only lived in Maerdy for two years, and that a century earlier.

In 1895, my Uncle John became a draper's apprentice at Porth in the Rhondda and three years later Daniel followed him there to train as a carpenter with Thomas and Evans, the company that made the popular carbonated beverage called Corona. Their mother longed to communicate directly with them but, even though she had been taught to read in Sunday school, she couldn't write; she had only had three months of schooling. During one visit to Llangeitho, John discovered a drawer full of papers bearing evidence of her attempting to write 'Dear John' and 'Dear Daniel' – proof of her desire to communicate with her sons without anyone else's assistance.

Daniel had quite a successful career as a carpenter in the Rhondda. Apart from a period in the South Wales Borderers during the First World War, he spent most of his career in Treorci. In 1934 he married Mary Potter, the daughter of William Potter, originally from Malvern in Worcestershire. William moved to Llandinam in Powys, where he looked after horses belonging to the coal magnate David Davies's family. It was that family's connections with the Rhondda that took him south, to work as a haulier, where he suffered an injury from a rockfall underground. As a consequence, he spent years in Bridgend Hospital – a terrible place according to his daughter, Mary; even passing through the town was dreadful to her, and the creation of the M4 came as a great relief.

My father, Daniel Davies, died when I was eleven years of age, but my mother, Mary, lived until I was in my fifties, and so she is the only one among my forebears whose memories I had the good fortune to be able to share.

She was born in Treorci in 1899. Her parents had died by the beginning of the First World War and Mary went to live with her mother's parents. Her mother, Anne, and also Anne's mother, Mary, were born either in Merthyr or in Rhondda Fawr. Mary was the daughter of Margaret and Evan Evans of Gilfachyrhalen, near New Quay, members of a family that had a strong sea-faring tradition. We owned an oil painting of a ship that Evan, the son of Evan Evans, had once captained (every sailor in the area was called a captain) – the same ship on which he drowned after a wreck off the coast of Tasmania in 1899. His brother David went to work in a shop in Pontypridd before going to run a farm called Ysguborwen and owned by two local spinsters in nearby Rhydfelen. David married the elder sister and they, in turn, had children.

When the elder sister died, it was the younger sister's responsibility to look after the children but David was not able to marry her because of a law, deriving from the precepts of the Church of England, that forbade marriage between a man and his deceased wife's sister. The Independents, unimpressed by Anglican edicts, were content to give their blessing to this second marriage, but I was surprised to learn that my old Auntie Nellie – a very respectable woman – was the product of a marriage not recognized by the state.

My grandmother, Anne, lived in Dowlais but she kept in close contact with her uncle David and it is little wonder that her daughter, my mother, considered the descendants of her great-uncle as her closest relatives. Anne eventually moved to Treorci and there she married Henry Davies, whose family had deep roots in Talyllychau, Carmarthenshire. According to the story, his forebears had taken part in the Rebecca Riots but, as the authorities closed in on them, they fled to Merthyr and from there moved on to the Rhondda. Henry Davies lived until my mother was in her twenties and therefore I heard more about him than any other member of his generation. Should anyone ask me where the roots of my family lie, I still answer every time: 'In Talyllychau'.

Henry Davies was an interesting man. He thought it beneath him to collect his pension of five shillings every week, considering it a paltry sum; instead, he would wait for a month, so that he could collect a full sovereign. He gave some of the money to his granddaughter and she used this to buy instalments of the *Children's Encyclopedia*; she kept every single copy in the series and I diligently read my way through the whole lot during the harsh winter of 1947. I thus feel that my interest in history, literature and landscape can be traced back to Arthur Mee. I am, therefore, hugely indebted both to Lloyd George's pension and to Henry Davies.

It seems that English was the language spoken at home when William Potter, my mother's paternal grandfather, was still alive – the Potter family grave, set among acres of Welsh headstones in Treorci graveyard, is almost the only one with an English inscription – and my mother turned back to English during her last weeks on earth. In her maternal grandfather's home, Carmarthenshire Welsh was spoken. However, some of her relatives and acquaintances spoke the Gwenhwyseg dialect and she remembered people in the Rhondda and in Aberdare saying things such as 'Shgwla pwy sy'n whilia', a localized way of saying 'Look who's talking'.

The focal point for migrants from the south-west was Bethlehem, the principal chapel of the Calvinistic Methodists, and that chapel was, in turn, the epicentre of the dialect spoken by people who had moved from those parts to Treorci. The Gwenhwyseg dialect, meanwhile, found sanctuary in the chapels of the Baptists and Independents, as their members were more likely to have roots in south-east Wales.

My mother was successful at Treorci Primary School, passing the eleven plus examination for Porth County, the only grammar school in the Rhondda. The family, however, couldn't afford to send her there and so she became a pupil at Pentre Sec – a school that could be reached without having to pay for bus travel. I have a collection of the school's set texts, among them the pupils' history book, *The History of England* by Arabella Buckley – a hagiography of the royal family and the empire. The school also taught a modicum of Welsh – *Hog Dy Fwyell* [Sharpen Your Axe] was its motto. My mother won first prize for Welsh when she was in the sixth form; the prize was a copy of the poems of Matthew Arnold. She was a promising pupil, especially in Mathematics and Physics and, despite serious problems with her eyesight, she gained the necessary qualifications to go to university. The family resources were not sufficient for this, but she had inherited enough money to attend training college. As she was very interested in her family connections with England, she chose to go to Exeter. Her grandfather found the idea of a young girl travelling through the Severn Tunnel and on into England with money in her pocket little short of horrifying, so he insisted that she stitched sovereigns into the tops of her stockings. When she arrived at the college and fumbled with her clothes, she was very surprised to see one of her fellow students signing a cheque to pay her fees. She was in college during the First World War and almost all the students were women; there was one lone male student among them – a wounded soldier – and everyone referred to him as Mr Man.

After becoming a certificated teacher, she considered taking a post in a school in south-west England, which she considered a most attractive area. However, because schoolteachers in the Rhondda had campaigned successfully for a decent income, wages were higher there than in rural areas. In addition, my mother had inherited a house in Treorci, a three-bedroomed house her father had bought at the end of 1890s for £280, which she sold for under £500 in 1945. She was appointed headmistress of Cwm-parc Primary School, where she had great success; she boasted that no one ever left her class without being able to read and write (English) and know their tables up to and including 12 x 12. By the time she finished at the school, she was responsible for the scholarship class, a year's hard graft for the pupils – a commitment that involved many set books. The favourite was *From Log Cabin to the White House*, the memoirs of James Garfield, the president of the United States, which explains, perhaps, the popularity of the name Garfield in the industrial communities of south Wales.

In a coal-mining area such as the Rhondda, the 1920s and 1930s were a period of incredible hardship and my mother helped out in shoe-exchange centres and worked tirelessly to give orphaned children a holiday. The Lord's Prayer was reworded by a young girl from Dowlais when she was on such a trip to Torquay. Instead of using the words 'Thy will be done on Earth as it is in Heaven,' she prayed that 'Thy will be done in Merthyr as it is in Devon'. Despite the times, those adults with a steady income and only a few daily expenses lived quite a good life. My mother went each Christmas to visit her relatives in Rhydfelen where 'May Treorcky' was seen as a poor relation of the family. When she married, the family in Rhydfelen gave her a complete dinner service to use at parties.

'Nobody holds dinner parties in Treorci,' she pointed out.

'They do in Rhydfelen,' came the reply. My mother insisted that Auntie Nellie attended my graduation ceremony, to prove that her family was just as good as her relatives.

My mother spent the Easter holidays in Somerset and Devon and adored such places as Lynmouth and Ilfracombe. The summer holidays saw some of her most adventurous holidaymaking and she was happy to spend up to half her year's salary on Lunn Poly tours. Almost every year she went to Paris or Brittany, Lucerne or Montreux, sleeping on the night ferry that carried trains in its hold across the Channel. She went to Basel in 1923, but noticing that inflation in Germany was very high, she crossed the border and stayed in the best hotel in Freiburg for next to nothing.

Her visit to Paris in 1927 was a key event in her personal history as it provided the spur which made her decide to relearn Welsh. She was there with her friend Blanche Thomas from Hawthorn, a Physics teacher at Abersychan Grammar School. (Roy Jenkins was among her pupils, a promising scholar in some subjects, though not in Physics.) Paris in 1927 was rabidly anti-American because of the decision by the United States to execute the anarchists Sacco and Vanzetti on the basis of the flimsiest of evidence against them. This attracted the ire of Einstein and George Bernard Shaw, which led to protests in a great many countries. It was believed that speaking English in France at the time was nothing short of dangerous, since it might give the impression that the speakers were from the United States. That was the opinion of the owner of the hotel where Blanche and Mary were staying – a man who had worked in Cardiff and had recognized their Welsh accents. 'If you can speak Welsh,' he advised them, 'do so.' Despite their chapel-going upbringing, they had little command of the language, and after struggling for hours, my mother decided to attend Welsh lessons on her return to the Rhondda.

She joined the Workers' Educational Association and met John Davies, who would become, later on, her brother-in-law, and who had been appointed the secretary of the movement in Wales in 1919 (he was the secretary for south Wales from 1925 onwards). By 1919 John had had many a career. After years of working in clothes' shops – dismal work in his opinion – he became a committed member of the Independent Labour Party, an official of the shopworkers' union and a correspondent for *Llais Llafur* [Labour Voice]. As his lungs were weak, he did not have to join the armed forces and spent the first part of the war working as an instructor with the YMCA. In 1917 he became the organizer of the Farm Workers' Union in west Wales and a colleague of the author D. J. Williams as he tried to establish the Labour Party in Pembrokeshire. James Griffiths had fond memories of him, and he tried to persuade Keir Hardie that there was a need for more of a Welsh slant to Labour's activities in Wales.

John's name was mentioned as a possible Labour candidate in Cardiganshire in 1918 but the party in the county did not have sufficient funds to back him and it was feared that his trenchant views about the wages of agricultural workers might enrage farmers in the area. (On the circumstances of the agricultural workers, see David Pretty's excellent book, *The Rural Revolt That Failed*.) Although sceptical of Marxism, he took pleasure in the fact that he was the only person who had read his way through the English translation of *Das Kapital* in Tonypandy library. He married Ruby from Somerset, a woman who was to stand as a Labour candidate in Wells in 1927. To anyone who knows the area, it is unnecessary to state that her attempt was unsuccessful. Many prominent people in Wales respected John Davies. W. J. Gruffydd noted in *Y Llenor* [The Literary Man]: 'After the death of John Morris-Jones and John Williams, Brynsiencyn, there was only one John left in Wales', and a booklet about him was published by the Gregynog Press following his death in 1937. John Davies's adherence to patriotic and progressive principles were an inspiration to me over many years, but I did not feel I was fully an heir to his political vision until I went to Pontrhydfendigaid in July 2007 to support the agreement between the Labour Party and Plaid Cymru to form the One Wales coalition government. (I wonder if the organizers of the meeting knew it was being held exactly seven hundred years after the death of Edward I?)

John died a few months before I was born and, therefore, only one name was ever considered for me. When I told my mother that I would have loved to have met my uncle, her answer was – bearing in mind the title of E. M. Forster's novel – 'You would have been a witness to his funeral, if there were such a thing as a "womb with a view".' John's widow was convinced he would be given a peerage when the Labour Party formed a government. She even suggested that he would persuade the authorities to ensure a 'special remainder' for me; the idea that I might have become a member of the House of Lords in my childhood is amusing. That said, I'm sure such a request would have been flatly rejected.

As a consequence of her membership of the Workers' Educational Association and Coleg Harlech, Mary Potter got to know John Davies well. She became even friendlier with his brother, Daniel. They were married in Bethlehem chapel, Treorci, in 1933, and a reception was held in Pontypridd in the company of the descendants of Mary's great-uncle David. They spent their honeymoon in Malvern and my mother recalled how she was given a shilling there by Harriet Potter, her monoglot English-speaking grandmother, for being able to pronounce the full name of Llanfairpwllgwyngyll.

Daniel and John were great companions. But Daniel was infuriated by John's insistence that he was, by dint of being the secretary of the Workers' Educational Association, a member of the working class while Daniel, with his carpentry workshop employing two people, was a member of the middle class. The difference between their lives was manifest. Not everyone would have thought it a matter of course, as John did on the occasion of my sister's birth, to note in a letter to the former secretary to the Cabinet: 'Last Thursday, I became an uncle.'

John lived in Wenallt Road, Rhiwbina, in a house that would be worth half a million pounds today, while Daniel lived in a terraced house in Treorci which had been inherited by his wife. John went on holiday with Thomas Jones to places such as Copenhagen, but the only foreign trip Daniel undertook was the crossing of the Negev desert during the campaign to take control of Jerusalem, when he contracted malaria, which weakened his constitution for the rest of his life. Every soldier who took part in the successful campaign to capture the city was given a medal, a decorated cross. I have no idea what my grandmother – a faithful attender at Daniel Rowland's chapel in Llangeitho – thought of this gift. I myself followed the route of the South Wales Borderers across the expanses of the Negev and it was interesting to discover a great many Welsh verses on gravestones in Beersheba – the graves of young men my father would surely have known. I especially liked the lines:

Hwyliodd yn wyn o Walia
Trwy y drin, wron da,
I hir saib ym Meersheba.

[He sailed pure from Wales
Through battle, a hero,
To a long rest in Beersheba.]

My mother had to resign her teaching post when she got married, because the Rhondda, in keeping with many other coal communities, defined careers almost without fail in masculine terms. (A friend of hers who was a teacher married in secret. Two years later she was dismissed for immorality, as it was believed that her visible pregnancy meant she would become an unmarried mother.) One of her friends concocted a fake advert for a job in a Rhondda school: 'Ability desirable; dedication optional; testicles essential.' When war broke out in 1939, the Director of Education for the Rhondda appeared at the door saying all the men had gone, so there was an opening for my mother. She spent the majority of the war years as a teacher in Penyrenglyn school, but in 1945 the Director was again at her door, this time informing her that the men had returned and so her job was disappearing. (Things have improved by now.)

The early years of the Second World War were very difficult for my father. The men he employed went into the army; he spent his nights fire-watching in Treorci and his workload grew even heavier because of the bomb damage in Cwm-parc. (He re-roofed the famous Parc and Dare Hall.) Because of overworking and the ongoing effects of malaria, he was almost bedridden by the end of hostilities.

There was no guarantee that the Rhondda, after the war, would allow married women to continue their duties as teachers, even if the woman was the only breadwinner in the family. By the end of the war, my mother was supporting four people, and yet her job was given to a young man half her age who lived with his parents.

Therefore, my mother's priority was to find an education authority that would give her the means to support her family. During the middle years of the war, she was offered the headship of the primary school in Tintinhull, a village near Yeovil in Somerset. A house was provided along with the post but when my father visited the place he concluded that it was too small to accommodate a family of four. I was very young at the time but I recall my father's reluctance to live in such a very English village. My father was very fond of a comment made about the Archbishop of Canterbury: 'Oh old Lang swine, how full of Cantuar!' Nowadays, not everybody understands this remark; Cantuar is the abbreviated form of the title of Archbishop of Canterbury, and Cosmo Lang held the post between 1928 and 1942. (It would have surprised my father greatly to hear of Welsh patriots these days who want to embrace the Anglican Church.)

Therefore, the idea of moving to Tintinhull was dismissed. I have subsequently visited the village and have often pondered what my fate might have been had the move taken place. It is a lovely area and Tintinhull is within easy reach of Montacute, one of the National Trust's best gardens. The school manager, the owner of the lovely gardens surrounding Tintinhull House, was also a powerful figure on the committee of Sherborne School and he suggested to my mother that I might be a pupil there some day. It is some relief to me that it never transpired.

We were living in Treorci throughout the Second World War and I look back at the terrible years between 1939 and 1945 with considerable longing. Every Saturday morning my sister and I would visit the Pavilion cinema, where we saw stirring films about the progress of the war. I remember particularly the images of water filling the streets of Rotterdam, with some of its citizens sailing through the city on upturned table-tops. In the afternoon, we would visit the park near the railway station, where there was a wealth of attractions. I very much admired the bushes and shrubs that grew there and relished the taste of the berberis leaves. I loved the Chilean pine that grew in front of Tremle, the only mansion in Treorci, and the lavender that flowed in profusion over the garden walls of Stuart Street. We would enjoy hugely the ventriloquism of Tomi Porthcawl, who performed in Bute Street, Treorci.

On Sundays we would go to Bethlehem chapel, where the children would be ushered into the English-language Sunday school when the Welsh-language sermon started. I enjoyed that school and I became skilled in the design of flat roofs made of felt, like the ones I believed were to be found in Palestine. The children were also expected to attend the Band of Hope, where we learned to climb, climb, climb in the song 'Dring i fyny yma, dring, dring, dring'. But because very few of us had much command of Welsh, what we actually sang was 'drink, drink, drink' – an entirely inappropriate chorus for a teetotal organization.

My mother remembered taking part in a procession, arranged by Bethlehem, to commemorate the lives lost on the *Titanic*, and she also recalled having to queue for over an hour to get a seat in the chapel gallery during the religious revival of 1904/05. She it was who introduced me to the revivalist Evan Roberts when I was in my early teens, when he was in his seventies and living in Rhiwbina near my Auntie Ruby. Even though her mother didn't wash the Sunday dinner dishes until the Monday, I do not think her daughter embraced such orthodox Christian values. Although she had heard thousands of sermons which underlined the primacy of faith, her favourite quotation was Bernard Shaw's dictum: 'Judge people not by their professed faith, but by the preconceptions on which they base their daily lives.'

I doubt also whether my father was a Christian – as it is defined by the faithful – even though he liked taking us to the Toc H eating house in Treorci, where its members enjoyed seeing me dress up in bus workers' and railway-men's hats. I feel fortunate not to have ministers of religion among my forebears. This allows me to be an atheist without fearing that I am 'shaming my fathers in their coffins'.

Later, I realized that more than a million people lived in the area between Pontypool and Llanelli, with the Rhondda at its heart. It was therefore an urban area almost as populous as Glasgow or Birmingham. But I best remember the rural corners. I dreamed that it was possible to chase after Germans through the forests of Tyle Du and Tyle Coch, and I was excited to learn that a bomb had fallen on Treorci's cemetery which was situated on the bare hills overlooking the town; I knew that this was the burial place of my mother's parents and I was very eager to see it. 'At best there will only be a skull there,' my mother said, but I felt that seeing my grandmother's skull would be a privilege in itself. My father would take me for walks to the heads of the Orci Vale, and once, when he was feeling particularly energetic, he took me to see the iron-age fortress of Maendy – the first of hundreds of ancient monuments I have visited.

I would paddle in the waters of the Rhondda Fawr river and imagine that the layer of small coal on the surface was a kind of chocolate. It was a delight to toboggan down the sides of the coal tips on trays and play hide-and-seek in the lush green fields of Glyncoli. There wasn't a single car in Dumfries Street and you could play right in the middle of the road. As everybody knew us, we could wander the hills without anyone being unduly concerned, as long as we were home before nightfall. The bomb shelters were splendid hiding places and clothes rationing turned out to be a blessing in disguise as it dispensed with having to make decisions about what to wear. We wore utility clothing, every garment bearing the motto 'Made in England', and we imagined that England was a factory located somewhere between Pentre and Porth. In Treorci itself, the place I loved the most was a shop in Bute Street belonging to Thomas Gower; the ceilings within the place supported a network of wires which carried pots of money from the point of sale to the cashier who would then send any change back along the wire.

By comparison with today, illnesses were legion in Treorci in the 1940s. Almost every man I knew bore the scars of the coal industry on his face, and my mother, whose family had suffered greatly in the wake of tragic events underground, felt happy when it was announced that a pit was to close – an attitude that was, truth be told, more commonly held than the rhetoric would suggest, certainly among women.

Many women suffered from goitre, my Auntie Rachel among them. It was worse for my Uncle Dai; he suffered from silicosis and spent hours walking from number 70 Dumfries Street to our house, number 59, as he would have to sit down to rest for a long period on many a window sill as he went, desperately trying to get his breath back. As he realized that his was not to be a long life, he filled up his back garden with the free coal the colliers received, so that his wife could be warm in her widowhood. Many of the children, meanwhile, wore callipers – the result of rickets, a consequence of the deprivations of the Depression.

Like most of my contemporaries, I had many illnesses: pneumonia, scarlet fever, rubella, mumps, bronchitis, chicken pox, measles, whooping cough and tonsilitis. I believe that the antibodies that developed within me during that period stood me in good stead for at least sixty years of good health. When I suffered from scarlet fever, I had to spend a period in the isolation unit at Tŷ'n Tila hospital. It was a blow to see my mother and Auntie Bet looking at me through the window, unable to come inside. It was an even greater blow that the hospital insisted on burning my cuddly panda before I left the place. (My sister avers that it was her panda in the first place.)

I visited Tŷ'n Tila again, this time at the request of Rhondda Cynon Taf council, to write a report about the only long house in the Rhondda (or *tŷ dau ben*, a two-end house, as it was called in Cardiganshire); it was hoped that the long house could be restored, along with the surrounding buildings, but the council's resources proved to be insufficient. On the occasion of this visit, I had lunch in the Cardiff Arms pub in Bute Street, Treorci. On hearing the accents around me I realized that, after many years, I had come home.

I started at Treorci Infants' School in 1942 when I was four years old. I have to confess that my friends and I pulled faces outside those houses not fortunate enough to contain a piano in the front room. We would also kick the buckets of coal dust that stood outside each house and chase the sheep that came down from the mountain to eat anything tasty in those buckets. My sister had started school in 1940, when the Rhondda abandoned its long-standing policy that a proportion of teachers – or, more likely women teachers – in infants' schools should speak Welsh. The occasional monoglot Welsh-speaking child was still making an appearance in the educational system of the Rhondda as late as the 1930s, but, by 1940 those teachers who had arrived along with the evacuees from London were the ones running the show. My sister had been raised in Welsh and could not therefore understand everything that was going on. My mother went to complain and was asked: 'Don't you know there's a war on, and that England is in danger?'

There is little doubt that this accounts for the fact that we heard English, mainly, at home. Even though half the adult population of Treorci spoke Welsh as recently as 1951, and kept a degree of connection with the Welsh chapels, at that time very few were concerned about the fate of the Welsh language in the Rhondda. I had a great many uncles and aunts – though there was scarcely one who was a blood relative – and the eldest among them were almost completely fluent in Welsh. Among my contemporaries, the only children who had any grasp of the language were those who spent their holidays in the Welsh-speaking villages from which their parents originally came. That was the case with Cennard Davies, and I remember him many years later talking about the disappointment he felt when he discovered that children in rural Carmarthenshire, where he had spent much of his childhood, now chose to converse with each other in English. I do not recall our hearing any Welsh at infants' school, and at the end of the schoolday we were expected to sing:

Now the day is over,
Night is drawing nigh;
Shadows of the evening
Steal across the sky.

The thing I remember especially about the infants' school was the 'Mickey Mouse' gas mask we were expected to carry with us to school each day and the dose of orange juice and cod liver oil we were given each morning. Food rationing was also interesting. Every individual was given a pint of milk each day, and because of people's desire to have everything to which they were entitled, more milk was drunk in the Rhondda during the war than in previous decades. In fact, the health of Rhondda people was better in 1945 than it was in 1939. Admittedly, we children found the rationing of sweets a bit of a nuisance, but old men (and there were plenty of those in Treorci) tended to leave their coupons in sweet shops. They had no use for them and therefore we had more than our share of chocolate and the like. Although travel was difficult, we had the thrill of visiting Barry, where we bathed in the sea and admired the barrage balloons floating above the docks. When I was three years old, we went on a holiday to Marcross, near St Donats, the first such event that I recall.

Two years later, we went to Aberaeron, travelling on the enchanting train from Treherbert to Blaengwynfi and on past Swansea, Llanelli, Cydweli Castle and Carmarthen, and then on the Aeron Valley railway from Lampeter to Aberaeron. It is a shame that we no longer have that pleasant line; I remember eagerly reciting the names of the last stations as we neared journey's end: Ciliau Aeron, Llannerch Aeron and Aberaeron. We met some of my mother's relatives who had remained in these parts, including my Uncle Jacob who kept bees near New Quay. We visited Llangeitho for the first time, to my father's great delight, as he hadn't been in the village where he spent his childhood for well over a decade. In Aberaeron my sister and I spent our time collecting hips and haws, the fruit of the rose and the hawthorn, as these berries, and the vitamins they contained, were considered essential to Britain's victory in the war.

Both the war and our period in the Rhondda were drawing to a close, but I am very conscious of the fact that my Rhondda upbringing has defined me for the rest of my days. We should not be nostalgic about the war, but I did miss the Rhondda very deeply, even though there were pastures new and all sorts of adventures ahead of me.

2

Bwlch-llan

1945–56

THE WAR IN Europe ended on 8 May 1945 (VE Day), and I well remember the big party held on Dumfries Street to celebrate. Particularly memorable were the bright lights outside the Parc and Dare Hall – a real show for someone like myself who hadn't seen lights in the street before. Soon the Treorci Italians were returning after their wartime incarceration on the Isle of Man and we were able to taste ice cream for the first time in the Sidoli family café. Between VE Day and the end of the war against Japan on 15 August 1945 (VJ Day), my mother got a permanent job as the headmistress of Bwlch-llan Primary School, about three miles from Llangeitho. We moved to Cardiganshire on VJ Day, travelling once again over the mountain to Blaengwynfi, and during the whole of the journey we witnessed parties in the street along with a sea of Union Jacks. (I was twelve before I saw *Y Ddraig Goch*, my first Red Dragon.)

As a member of the family was now involved in education in Cardiganshire (many others among us were destined to do likewise), and others were involved in agriculture, or had been sailors, or lead miners, I realized that my family had helped to contribute to what were seen as the four pillars of the county's economy. My mother was extremely successful as the headmistress of Bwlch-llan, as the current

Ceredigion Council Chief Executive, Bronwen Morgan, and the educationalist John Albert Evans have testified. I can bear witness to it myself, as she gave me what was to be my only formal education over a period of four years. I wistfully remember her ability to turn the stories of the Old Testament into enchanting adventures. By the time I was eleven years of age, I was so thoroughly schooled in numeracy that I could have dazzled in O level examinations on the subject. My mother's greatest interest was what she described as mathematical puzzles – a combination of logic and algebra.

I doubt whether Bwlch-llan would have been a natural first choice for my mother. As she was used to the urban life of Treorci, it was hard for her to cope with life in a village which had a total of only seven houses. She was disappointed to see the range of goods on offer in its two shops. (John Albert, in his autobiography, *Llanw Bwlch*, tells an entertaining story about his attempt to buy some toilet paper in one of the shops.) My mother had also got used to taking trains and buses and it was a shock to live in a village without even a bus stop, but even worse was the lack of electricity or drinking water in the house. Electricity was unfamiliar to everyone, and I remember people coming to the mart in Tregaron and attempting to light a cigarette from a light bulb. When maintaining small rural schools became an issue, I do not recall her expressing strong views on the matter. I received a phone call asking me to start a petition when there were rumours that some rural schools in the county were under threat of closure.

'Why?' I asked.

'Because they're there,' came the reply.

I doubt whether my mother would ever have signed such a petition. As the headmistress, for more than twenty years, of a one-teacher school, she could go a month or more without encountering another adult during her work hours.

I had similar experiences; there were only eighteen children in Ysgol Bwlch-llan and only infrequently did a pupil go on from there to a secondary school. When I went to Tregaron County School I did not know how to interact with my contemporaries; I learned how to enjoy being by myself, a condition I seem to appreciate increasingly.

But any doubts about living in Bwlch-llan evaporated because of the generosity of our neighbours. We wandered every path in the parish of Nancwnlle and there was a ready welcome for us in every house. From the back of Tŷ'r Ysgol (or Ael-y-bryn, as everyone called it), we could see at least twenty farms and I realized that we had had tea or supper in each and every one of them.

The generosity of the local inhabitants was noteworthy. Every October the people who lived in houses without land would be a given a supply of *cig mân*, those parts of the pig which could not be salted. John Davies the Shop was so fond of *cig mân* that he had to spend each November taking the spa waters in Llanwrtyd Wells to get over the effects of his feasting. In the winter of 1947 some of our neighbours trudged through the deep snows to Bronnant after hearing a rumour that there was bread there that they could carry home to their neighbours. The politeness of our neighbours, too, was pretty much proverbial. If we owed anyone any money, nobody called simply to present a bill. It was necessary to give the impression that the visit was purely social and the bill appeared after an hour or two of conversation, just before the visitor sidled out the door.

I remember a new neighbour asking if the locals had a word equivalent to the Spanish *mañana*. The reply came that there was no word that conveyed the same urgency of action. An old woman lived by herself in the village; she went each day from house to house, where she would enjoy two full meals in exchange for turning the pages of the *Welsh Gazette* into spills for lighting the fire. The *Welsh Gazette* was our newspaper – the publication that supported Llewelyn Williams against Lloyd George's candidate in the Cardiganshire by-election of 1921. I remember congratulating Geraint Howells and his wife after some radical action or other on their part. 'Remember,' said she, 'that our forebears were Llewelyn Williams's people.' After the demise of the *Welsh Gazette* we had to make do with the *Cambrian News*.

I never saw a single sign of the alleged miserliness of Cardiganshire people, even though many a Cardi has been on the receiving end of references to this tightfistedness. Mari James, Llangeitho's favourite story concerned a tramp who wandered the Teifi Valley. He would gather cow manure from the fields and go the door of a farmhouse asking for some salt to put on the cowpat he was about to eat, to give it a bit more flavour. When he was on the Carmarthenshire side of the river, the farmer's wife would be shocked and she would invite the tramp inside for a square meal. On the Cardiganshire side, the farmer's wife would comment, 'Don't eat that manure; we've got some fresh stuff in the shed.'

The majority of Bwlch-llan's inhabitants were confirmed Liberals – a rather empty political creed in my father's opinion. On the cusp of voting for the first time, I asked a Liberal county councillor what his policy was concerning primary schools and bilingual road signs, and his answer was, 'My father, my uncle and grandfather were county councillors, therefore I don't have to answer a question from a young whippersnapper.' Roderic Bowen, the Liberal MP for Cardiganshire, feared that the Conservatives would field a candidate against him, and so the substance of his speeches in the village was an attack on all shades of socialism. (In those days each candidate was expected to speak before an audience in every village.)

'A Labour government', he suggested in 1955, 'will be sure to attempt to nationalize the land.'

'Who will assess the value of our farms?' asked one of the poorest smallholders in the village.

'The valuer from Carmarthen, more than likely', came the reply.

'Very well', said the smallholder. 'He's a very fair person and we are sure to get a very significant sum.'

A slightly paranoid Roderic Bowen described his visit to Poland: 'There were hidden microphones in every room listening in on our conversations.' Rumour had it that he got hold of a spanner and went to find and disconnect the listening devices; he dismantled one he found in the middle of the floor and a chandelier fell on top of a group of people having a dinner party in the room below.

There was little sympathy for the Conservative Party in the village. They enjoyed the story about the local squire, Rogers-Lewis of Abermeurig Hall, who arrived with his groom to cast his vote in Bwlch-llan school during the elections of 1885. Rogers-Lewis was slightly stunned to see that his groom was also voting but he had to accept that parliamentary reforms meant that his servant had acquired the right to do so.

'Who got your vote?' he asked.

'The Liberals,' came the answer.

'I voted for the Tory', said Rogers-Lewis. 'It would have been better if the two of us had stayed at home.'

The family who resided at Abermeurig Hall was one of two 'aristocratic' families who lived in our area. The other was the Hext Lewes family, who lived in Llanllŷr, Talsarn. They had a large glasshouse and grew grapes. I well remember a woman from the Aeron valley, famous for the wine she made from elderflowers, asking him, 'Could you make wine from grapes?' When Hext Lewes rode across her garden, his dogs in tow, yelling 'Tally Ho!' she corrected him, shouting, '*Nid talu 'to, talu nawr'* which means 'Not pay some other time, pay now.' Mrs Hext Lewes ran a branch of the Girl Guides in the hall but only English-speaking girls were invited to join. It was rumoured that one of the Lewes family had joined the Labour Party on his deathbed, as he felt that if he was going to go, it was better for the departed to leave as one of 'them' rather than one of 'us'.

My parents stuck with the Labour tradition of the Rhondda. When Aneurin Bevan said: 'The Tories are lower than vermin', one of them asked, 'Why is the man being so kind about them?' My parents insisted I should be in the Rhondda during Vesting Day, 1 January 1947, when private ownership of coal mines came to an end. Later, I came to realize that I was, above all, a child of the Attlee government. There was a tendency to depict this period of government as an Age of Poverty but we who enjoyed our childhood during it remember receiving all manner of new things – oranges one day, bananas the next, grapes the following week and then, capping it all, Penguin chocolate biscuits, which you were able to buy without coupons.

The greatest achievement of the period was the establishment of the National Health Service in 1948, a daring feat when one remembers that the national debt as a proportion of GDP was higher then than now. The authors of the scheme were Aneurin Bevan and James Griffiths, who were building, in turn, on the work of David Lloyd George; as a consequence, an adherence to principles of social justice became absolutely central to Welsh values.

I was treated for appendicitis in 1951, a treatment for which, I suspect, my parents could not have afforded to pay in the days before the establishment of a free health service. In 1945, in our first month in Bwlch-llan, a great many people came to the house bringing money to pay for the right to a bed at Aberystwyth hospital. My mother found these payments astonishing – she had grown used to the loosely termed welfare state that existed in the Rhondda – but she sent the money on to the hospital; as a rural headmistress, she was expected to be an unpaid welfare officer. My mother was also in charge of electoral polling in the village and therefore felt that she should say nothing in public about her political allegiances. She never intimated how she voted, although I am convinced she voted for the interesting Labour candidate, Iwan Morgan, in 1950; then for the brilliant candidate David Jones-Davies in 1955 and for Elystan Morgan in 1966. (I have the distinct feeling that in the last election in which she cast her vote, she backed Cynog Dafis.) As she was very keen to ensure we understood the polling system, she insisted that we got to school by seven o'clock on election day to see that the voting box was empty, before a policeman from Aberaeron arrived to seal it with red wax.

The greatest source of pleasure for me was the beauty of the countryside and the rich profusion of wild plants. I went almost every day to Pen-y-gaer, where there was a stunning view of the Aeron valley, and I learned where to find all the wild flowers in the area – bluebells, wood anemones, marsh marigolds, cotton grass, cowslips and marsh orchids. A chestnut tree grew near Cwmeiarth, a Chilean pine near Fron-goch, and a wealth of bilberries along the banks of Cwm Llethr Hir. I knew where to spot red squirrels and where to hear the curlew and the cuckoo sing – birds which no longer grace the spring in the area. Almost everything I remember about Bwlch-llan is encapsulated in the poem 'Fern Hill'. Like Dylan Thomas, I too had seen 'The night above the dingle starry' and 'I lordly had the trees and leaves/Trail with daisies and barley/Down the rivers of the windfall light'.

I sometimes imagined that I was living within the covers of one of Arthur Ransome's books; my home was Swallowdale – the valley between Tŷ'n Celyn and Pont-gou – and that's where

I taught my pigeons to carry messages, like the characters in *Pigeon Post*. I admired Dick in *Winter Holiday* as he rescued a sheep from a ledge but then I realized that the story was a rewording of the poem 'Pwllderi'. The spur to action for the poet Dewi Emrys was not the smile in the market place but, rather, the bleat of relief as the animal was saved, and I could say the same for a legion of shepherds who worked the hilly slopes of Mynydd Bach.

I came to delight hugely in gardens, especially the lovely one owned by Miss Herbert, Arfryn. I had experimented with growing lettuce from seed in the Rhondda but there was enough land at Ael-y-bryn to be more adventurous. I developed a heather garden, a rockery, and borders of shrubs and flowers, and I was greatly inspired by Enid Blyton's instructions on how to plant perennials in April and bulbs in September. I got hold of the extensive catalogues produced by the Hillier company and imagined I would be a landscape architect when I grew up.

As she knew precious little about agriculture, my mother came to the conclusion that it would be possible to learn something by listening to *The Archers*, a programme to which we remained faithful (apart from a period when there was conflict with *Teulu Tŷ Coch*) right from the beginning of the series up to the present day. The radio became very important to us. In a house without electricity, we needed a dry battery and a wet battery. The former would last up to three months, but in its last weeks it would be put in the oven in order to squeeze a few additional minutes out of it; the latter would need replenishing every ten days or so, a task which required it being carried to Felin-fach where there was already an electricity supply. When the radio broadcasts fell silent on the occasion of the death of King George VI, my mother's only comment was, 'The wet battery has given up the ghost'. We lived on the border between SWEB and MANWEB and neither company had much interest in us.

Electricity was not the only thing we lacked. In 1945 only two local families owned a car, while the post office was the only place with a telephone, and that inside, not in a kiosk. Our neighbours proved themselves to be inventive in the ways they kept in touch with each other. A train brought one-day-old chicks to Tregaron; they were picked up by the driver of the school bus who then brought them to us. My mother would place a red sheet where any potential purchaser of the chicks could see them and bring a horse and cart to collect them.

I grew to love the character of the community living above the Vale of Aeron. The local people still used the names of individual fields – an important source of history, as was the naming of parts of the roads: Pen Llethr Hir, meaning head of the long hill, while others carried people's names, or other insights, such as Pen-lôn-speit, Ffynnon Caradog [Caradog's Well] and Pen-lôn Penherber, the top of Penherber's Lane.

I much enjoyed reading David Jenkins's book about south Cardiganshire society as it was at the beginning of the twentieth century. I was familiar with pretty much everything he described, such as the tendency for the owner of the local bull to be also the principal deacon in his chapel; the way in which the owners of fields were only too happy to give seed potatoes and cattle manure to smallholders on condition that they, in turn, help with the potato harvest in the autumn; and the tendency for the children of freeholding parents not to marry – the key, perhaps, to the fall in the number of children in the area. There were over two hundred children in Ysgol Bwlch-llan in 1900, when the majority of local inhabitants were tenants, while there were only fifteen in 1965 when the majority of parents owned their own farms.

The greatest blessing of my time in Bwlch-llan was my

immersion in the Welsh language. The children of the village ensured I should be completely fluent in it – an experience not dissimilar to that of the poet Waldo Williams in Mynachlog-ddu. I also had very long conversations with some of the old ladies who lived locally, especially Letitia Lodwick. She used to say things like '*Paid â 'mél â'r ridens 'na*' [Don't fiddle with those curtains] and she would be tickled pink by my use of terms such as '*neisied*', the Treorci word for 'handkerchief'. At auctions we heard words such as *sopyn* [small stack or bundle] and *helem* [cornrick], and by comparison with the dull names of the farms around Ambridge, the names of farms in Cardiganshire were full of imagination. Their owners eschewed the habit of adding 'farm' as a suffix to the original name, a habit which has become increasingly popular nowadays.

Our neighbours' attitude towards Welsh was perplexing. The language reigned over the area and the evacuees who had come to live there during the war were entirely fluent. At the end of the 1940s, there were only two English families in the district and they did not stay long. When a non-Welsh-speaking family moved to Bwlch-llan, the older inhabitants would tend to say they doubted if they would see their gravestones hereabouts. But nobody thought it odd that the instructions on the telephone told the user to 'Dial the number you want' in English, while the Welsh instructions explained into which hole you should place your finger and in which direction you should turn the dial. Indeed, there were some who believed that the telephone wires were unable to carry Welsh at all.

A local who had returned after a stint as a teacher in Cardiff placed a sign, '*paent glwyb*', on his gate, a warning that the paint was wet; this caused derision among his neighbours, who had never seen anything but the English version of such a notice. Matters of ethnicity and class manifested themselves in the choice of words: English or Welsh. To our neighbours, shoes were worn on special occasions while *esgidiau* were for working in; a cake made at home was a *cacen* but you bought cakes in shops. This was a phenomenon I also noted in Brittany; the only advertisement I saw in Breton was one extolling the quality of working clothes.

But even if the good people of Bwlch-llan had an ambivalent attitude towards Welsh, they were nevertheless custodial in their care of the language. Listening to stories about the Bwci Bwlch, the White Lady and corpse candles was an untrammelled pleasure. The members of the local Young Farmers' Club were all faithful to the language, of course, while there was enthusiastic attendance at night classes organized by the Extra-Mural department of UCW Aberystwyth. Many social meetings were held, often with an element of competition, and one of the best ways to learn verse was to sit through some of the competitions which had no preliminary rounds and absorb tens of performers reciting *'Cloch y Llan'* [The Parish Bell], or *'Gwelais ei fen liw dydd'* [I saw his wagon by day] or the poem about two rabbits, *'Dwy gwningen fechan'*. Longer verses featured as well, and being present during the hymn-singing contest for those over fifty years of age was a good way to learn some of the very best works of hymn writers such as William Williams, Pantycelyn, and Ann Griffiths.

The chapel was a hub for the Welsh language. Those frequenting the place had a fear of anything that smacked of ritual and therefore baptisms were held in the vestry, although, interestingly enough, marriages and funerals were held in the chapel itself. Inside, families would sit together in their usual pews, while in the vestry men would sit on the right and women on the left. Children would sit with their mothers, and the Bwlch-llan equivalent of the bar mitzvah was the passage of a boy from the left side to the right. Another sign of the distrust of ritual was the absence of any service whatsoever at Christmas and on Good Friday. (Village children had hardly any Christmas presents but they could benefit substantially from *calennig*, money given out on New Year's Day). Churchgoers were suspicious of the south Cardiganshire habit of arranging eisteddfodau on Good Friday. By now, however, every sign of interdenominational tension has disappeared, not because of the growth of mutual understanding but because the increase in the number of incomers has left the inhabitants of the county's villages believing that such divisions have little to do with them.

As there were so few surnames in the area – Jones, Davies, Evans or Morgan formed almost the entire range – there was a habit of adding the house name to the baptismal name: Jac Fron-Goch, Anne Bwlch, Mari Ardwyn and so on. Because I came from outside the village I needed another handle. As I was eager not to dismiss small centres of population, I insisted I lived in Bwlch-llan. As a consequence, I became known as John Bwlch-llan, a name of which I am not overly fond, as others have deeper roots in the village than my own, and therefore a better claim to the name.

We left the village very seldom, principally because my father, by the 1940s, was unable to climb the steep hill to the village. But we did leave sometimes and I remember our jaunt to Llyn Eiddwen with real pleasure. We went to visit my father's relatives, including Dic in Pontrhydfendigaid, the son of the sister of William Davies who had been killed in 1885; I met William's sister, a woman who had had no connection with her brother's family for over sixty years. On the occasion of that visit we went to Strata Florida Abbey, a genuinely exciting experience.

From time to time we would hire a car and go to visit my father's cousin, Auntie Martha, in Llan-non – the great-grandmother of Huw Lewis who chaired Cymdeithas yr

Iaith Gymraeg, the Welsh Language Society. Her daughter Jennie taught me how to harvest periwinkles, shellfish that used to be eaten more widely in Wales and during the famine in Ireland. I like the story about Máirín de Valera, a scholar and expert on marine life who spent a great deal of her time gathering samples on the coasts of Clare and Galway. For the locals, this was proof positive that her father, Éamon de Valera, the prime minister of Ireland, was too mean to feed his daughter properly, and as a consequence he lost a good deal of his electoral support. Elsie, Jennie's sister, introduced me to seabirds. I well remember her showing me a tern carefully feeding its chick. 'That's as it should be,' she said. 'Every good tern deserves a mother.'

My father tried to do what he could; he planted vegetables in the garden and he would accompany me on a visit to Allt-y-gaer to cut hazel sticks to support our pea plants as they grew. He took great pride in my increasing articulacy in Welsh and my success in the eleven plus examinations. He also kept up his interest in world affairs, and grew to fear the growing interrelationship with the United States following the establishment of NATO. He took pride in the readiness of local chapels to organize memorial services for Gandhi. As he had been to Jerusalem, he was considered an expert on Palestine and the developments there. My father went to chapel sometimes, but his heart sank when visitors came on a Sunday to enquire who was ill, as no-one had been present in the congregation. But among the majority of our friends and neighbours, a belief in God was unshakeable. I remember the principal deacon, during one dry spell in the 1940s, praying for rain. Huge storms followed during the week, to which the deacon responded by saying: 'I'd like to thank you for the rain; I know I asked for it, but I had thought you'd use a little more common sense.'

My mother derived a great deal of pleasure from the

occasional *seiat*, or chapel meeting, especially those addressed by Mrs Jones, Bwlch-graig, a woman who was still profoundly under the influence of the spiritual awakening of 1904/05. On the other hand, she did not derive much pleasure from Sunday school, which she dismissed as an opportunity for the older generation to berate people for turning their backs on the old ways.

We tended to go for a walk on Sunday afternoons and, as we met those who were on their way home after chapel, we would often hear the comment: 'Don't you realize which day of the week it is?' My mother insisted we hide behind a wall or hedge when we saw chapel-folk approaching, an undignified action which led to my hating Sundays and dismissing all forms of organized Christianity. My atheism came as some surprise to one of my neighbours. 'How on earth,' she asked, 'can you eat meat if you don't believe in God?' – a comment that has perplexed me ever since. I am increasingly convinced that religion is the worst curse on our contemporary world; perhaps the secularization of Europe holds the key to the survival of the peoples of the earth – if we accept that they will, indeed, survive.

It is hard to understand nowadays the way in which Calvinist Methodism presided over life in parts of Cardiganshire in the 1940s. I remember two farmers on the bus going to Lampeter discussing the Doctrine of the Atonement, while some of the villagers owned the complete works of Calvin. It was expected that the head teacher of the village school should also organize the Sunday school, while county councillors would tell candidates for posts in the secondary schools: 'I'm sure you're a full member (of the chapel).' On *Diwrnod y Pwnc*, when the congregation would recite long passages of the Bible in unison, the doors of the county's schools would be shut. When *Diwrnod y Pwnc* was held in Llangeitho, I got into a great deal of trouble by leading children from Bwlch-llan Sunday school to paddle in the river Aeron in their best clothes.

The highlight of the year was the Sunday school trip, and the photograph of members of Bwlch-llan chapel sitting on Barmouth beach in June 1947 has subsequently appeared in almost every *papur bro* (Welsh-language community newspaper) in Cardiganshire. I like the story about one chapel's outing in particular. The plan was to go to Mumbles, but the driver misheard and took them to Tumble. The travellers had a whale of a time, not least because the inhabitants of Tumble, a coal-mining village, were so thrilled that so many people had come to visit that they went out of their way to welcome them. The outing was a roaring success and I heard that, as a consequence, the chapel organized an annual visit to Tumble for a decade and more.

My mother considered making an application for a job in the far south of the county; most of the inhabitants were Unitarians and a bus ran through the village.

'You cannot live there,' she was told. 'The inhabitants don't believe in the Trinity and they all buy Sunday newspapers.'

'I like the *Observer*,' my mother replied.

'I wasn't thinking about the *Observer*,' came the reply. 'Think about that woman who stays in bed all day Sunday reading the *News of the World*. But there you are, she belongs to the Church.'

My mother, meanwhile, was warming towards the Church, possibly because she, like the politician Cynog Dafis, wanted to escape the tyranny of the sermon. Every Sunday morning we heard the sons of Pen-gaer ringing the lovely bells of the church of St Gwynlle. The church itself has been closed and turned into a house bearing the name Dunroamin. Behind the house one can see the ancestral graves of the family of historian Hywel Teifi Edwards and his broadcaster son, Huw.

One of the merits of living in Bwlch-llan was the impossibility of buying London newspapers there. I would see them on a visit to Lampeter and would be astonished at the vitriolic attacks of the right-wing newspapers on the Attlee government. My father liked a rhyme he read in one of the left-wing papers:

If you want the river of truth to run both bright and clear,
You'll have to damn the Beaverbrook and drain the Rothermere.

In 1949 I embarked on six years' attendance at Tregaron County School. Each year, the pupils would be taken to the statue of the pacifist Henry Richard in the centre of the town. In those days an old man often sat in front of the Memorial Hall and he would scowl at us before explaining that he didn't warm at all to this pacifism. He admitted enjoying taking part in the First World War, as it was the only time he'd been able to get away from his wife.

Compared with the pleasures of primary school, I did not greatly enjoy secondary school. This was partially explained by the hour-long trip to school, with another hour's journey back home. Though the bus travelled through some beautiful countryside, it was at least a year before I could travel on it without being sick.

But the main problem was the school's emphasis on team sports. The pupils of some of the larger primary schools – Tregaron and Pontrhydfendigaid, for example – were long used to this sort of activity, but it was entirely alien to me, and I had no desire whatsoever to take part. I found that I could leave school at the end of Wednesday morning and avoid the afternoon's sporting activities altogether. I would spend the time walking to Rhiw Dywyll in Cwm Berwyn or walking the moorlands at Blaencaron – lovely experiences which got me out of rugby, football and cricket entirely. Those of us who do not understand the rules of such ball games and do not watch team sports of any description, are isolated, in today's Wales, from almost all connection with a great number of our contemporaries. Not watching rugby and soccer on television or, indeed, avoiding watching anything at all on television, gives you many hours of freedom to do other things, which tend to be more interesting by far.

Half a century on from my own schooldays, I ponder deeply about the place of education in our lives. As dedicated listeners to the Home Service on our radio set, we often heard members of the English working class explaining why they didn't feel they could aspire to further education; the same is still being said by some people today. Such sentiments were, and are, entirely alien to me. In Bwlch-llan (and even more so in the Rhondda), people took it for granted that those who did well at school were likely to progress to some form of higher education. One of the poorest families in the area lived at Pen-gaer, yet no one was surprised when the son of the family, George Noakes, became the Archbishop of Wales. Mrs Thomas, Lôn, had only one field and one cow, but her son's success as a doctor was considered to be entirely natural. I came to the conclusion that our educational aspirations were set higher in Wales than they were in England – even though every scholarly success meant the area would be deprived of another talented young person.

The desire for education was manifest also in the emphasis on learning the piano. There was a woman in the village who derived all of her income from teaching the instrument and I had to attend her lessons in the chapel vestry. Even though my mother had no interest in music, she believed her inability to play the piano had impeded her career at Cwm-parc. The worst time of my childhood was the daily half-hour when she would insist I should practice the piano, so that I could eventually accompany singers. As a consequence, I took against songs themselves, a feeling that has remained with me for decades. Therefore, other than the occasional discussion programme (normally on Sunday evenings) Radio Cymru's preference for broadcasting popular songs annoys me. It seems that this is part of a strategy to attract younger listeners, although I know young people whose interests are far more wide-ranging. I do not understand why attention is skewed towards young people's needs when it comes to radio. So many of them are steeped in visual culture that it is impossible for them to appreciate the appeal of this much more economical medium. Listeners to better-quality programming tend to be older and the ageing population happens to be the sector of society that is growing most quickly. Perhaps there is a concern that these are the very people who are edging nearer death. However, I remember that Beatrice Webb, writing in 1920, observed that the only people who attended church in Russia were old women dressed in black. The same comment was made by Laurens van der Post in 1954 and by *Newsweek* in 1985. It may be that all the comments are correct, but it is most unlikely that they were the same old ladies in every case. Therefore, if Russian churches can recruit generation after generation, surely quality radio programmes can do the same. It was interesting to read the case for a commercial Radio 1 station in Welsh in *Golwg* [View] magazine. That would release resources within the BBC to maintain a Welsh service with similar content to that available in English on Radio 4 – even though that outlet, too, is weaker than it used to be.

I had attended Tregaron school for six months when my father died on 9 March 1950. I remember every minute of that night – my mother waking us up, before going to ring for the doctor. To do this it was necessary to wake Mair Post (Mair Lloyd Davies, who later became prominent in the world of the eisteddfod) to use the telephone. Mair returned with my mother to the house, where she was particularly interested in the temperature of the dead body. During the next three days, every one of our neighbours came to call and my mother had to describe the details to each caller. It is possible that this practice derives from the cohesion of the community, but the erosion of the custom has no doubt been a relief to many. My father was buried alongside his mother and brother in the family grave in Llangeitho and, as the only son, I had to throw the first shovel-full of soil onto the coffin. Auntie Nellie and Auntie Ruby came to stay with us and Ruby noted that my father, who died little more than four months after reaching the age of sixty-five, had received very little of his state pension. (My mother fared better, receiving a pension for over thirty years.) Ruby, my father's sister-in-law, was of the opinion that she should adopt my sister Anne – quite a common practice among childless women in that period; my mother curtly refused – the beginning of a breach that would eventually become complete.

Even though we grieved for him, I do not think my father's death led to a fundamental change in our circumstances. I came to know someone for whom a parent's death was an unbearable loss, but that was not the case for me. My sister and I were totally confident that my mother would be able to provide comfortably for us, which she did. When the secondary school arranged a visit to Paris in 1952, we could both rest assured that she would be able to pay for us to go.

I remember every detail of our first visit to the continent – even the name of the ship that carried us across the Channel. After seeing Versailles, the Eiffel Tower and the Louvre, I vowed to spend a portion of each and every year travelling in Europe – an intention I have realized over a period of more than sixty years.

But I felt increasingly that I should be seeing more of Wales. By the time I was fourteen, an excellent teacher, Mari Boden, had inspired me by interpreting two anthologies of poetry, namely *Y Flodeugerdd Gymraeg* [The Welsh Anthology] and *Beirdd Ein Canrif* [The Poets of Our Century]. I still remember her analysis of R. Williams Parry's poem about the curlew, 'Y Gylfinir' (a bird we called *'chwibanogl'* locally). As I felt queasy trying to read on the school bus, I found it was easier to spend the time commiting poetry to memory, and soon I had memorized most of the content of both these books. I was disappointed by the snide attitude of a number of teachers in Tregaron – including Welsh speakers – towards Welsh-language literature, and I started to read the volumes of writers such as Thomas Parry. The school's use of Welsh was interesting, and I had many experiences which showed that one could live in a Welsh-speaking area and grow up to be an adult before realizing that many of one's teachers spoke the language. Very likely I would not have welcomed more emphasis on the Welsh language in my early teens, as I was still not completely fluent. I won the chair in the school eisteddfod – the first person, I believe, to do so with a poem in English. The shadow of English lay over me, and after visiting Malaysia, Turkey, India and Germany, I realized that I shared this condition with many other people in the world. I remember a guide separating tourists into groups outside a palace in Istanbul.

'Turkish here; English there,' he said.

'But we are Germans,' shouted the leader of a large tour group.

'Germans,' said the guide, 'is English.'

I spoke to the German tourists and not one of them had the least difficulty in following the English commentary.

My chair-winning poem was patriotic, and getting to know Wales became something of an obsession. My mother would take us every year to stay in Aberystwyth and she arranged for us to be taken on trips to such places as the summit of

Snowdon and St Davids. Legend had it that there was a green space near Borth where one could sunbathe in the nude. We were not taken there. Apparently, a student from Spain was given the opportunity to visit the place. As he left, he only said one word, the Spanish for thank you, *gracias*. Several times a year we enjoyed the hospitality of Auntie Nellie in Rhydfelen and Auntie Ruby in Rhiwbina and I therefore got to know the area I considered to be my own, the south-east. I visited Castell Coch, Caerffili, Caerleon, Caerwent, Newport (especially the Transporter Bridge), Merthyr and Cardiff. My Auntie Nellie was horrified when I told her about my visit to Bute Street in Cardiff. 'Even policemen have to walk there in threes', she told me.

I felt that I should expand my horizons somewhat, so I joined the Youth Hostels' Association and I believe I have stayed in every hostel in Wales. I hitch-hiked from place to place and the first hostel I visited was Kings, near Dolgellau. By the time I was eighteen I had visited nearly every parish in Wales; there were over a thousand of them, prior to their dissolution in 1974. By the time I set about the business of writing a history of Wales, I had come to agree entirely with J. E. Lloyd's comment that the main prerequisite of a historian was mud on one's shoes.

The staff at Tregaron school included many brilliant educators and I wondered, as did Goronwy Rees, why so many gifted people should undertake such a thankless task. I remember, with respect, the talents of Coleman Porter, the Chemistry teacher and dear Eirlys Watkin Williams, who taught History. Nevertheless, I tend to agree with Charles Arch that some of the teachers were a bit listless. Incidentally, a dozen of my contemporaries from south Cardiganshire have published autobiographies. Are we that interesting?

Dan Jones, Mari James, Llangeitho's brother, was an even more gifted teacher than Mari Boden and under his influence I fell in love with English literature. Reading Wordsworth made me a pantheist – I sometimes went to Pen-y-gaer to kneel down and worship the sunset. Later on, I was astonished at the WJEC's selection of books for the English examinations. We studied *Badger's Green, South with Scott* and *Memories of a Fox-Hunting Man*, and it was only years later that I realized that people in Wales had written literature of merit in English. The exception was the publicity given to Dylan Thomas when he died; the sixth form in Tregaron school sent a contribution to the *Western Mail*'s fund to bring the body back to Wales from America.

My period at Tregaron school came to end, more or less, at the beginning of the summer of 1955. I had not, as yet, received the results of my A level examinations but my teachers were confident I would receive the necessary grades to go to university. I did not want to make any decision when I was just seventeen, so I spent six weeks hitch-hiking across Europe. I went to Abermeurig Hall, where Rogers-Lewis, as a magistrate, signed my passport application form, before going to the bank to buy £20 in travellers' cheques, along with a few thousand francs – a pound was worth a thousand francs in those days.

As I travelled I saw wonders in the city of Bruges. Drivers in Belgium liked stopping at bars, and they would offer me a glass of beer, but I did not acquire a taste for it then. I rose early to enjoy the first service of the day in the cathedral at Reims and later fell asleep in the car in which I was given a lift. I was dropped off in the countryside of Lorraine and slept in a hay barn, managing to reach Strasbourg by the end of the morning. As I strolled through that beautiful city, I noticed that the majority of its inhabitants spoke a version of German but that everywhere there were posters which proclaimed: '*Parlez Francais; c'est plus chic.*'

I crossed the river Rhine and, as I travelled towards the

Black Forest, I formulated a list of instructions for hitch-hikers. Here they are:

Never go to sleep.

Never walk in the direction you wish to travel, because every time you pass another hitch-hiker you are reducing your chance of getting a lift.

Young women should carry a hatpin, especially in Italy.
(This was the suggestion of my cousin Mair from Rhydfelen.)

A young man should give the impression that he understands nothing, should the conversation stray into unfamiliar territory.

The sleeping-bag you carry should not be too big.

Do not smoke at the side of the road – although you might be lucky if the driver going past needs a light for his cigarette.

I arrived at a hostel in Freiburg which was attractively situated in the middle of a wood. There, I discovered that my travellers' cheques and my return ticket for the boat had slipped out of my pocket in one of the cars I had been travelling in. (The driver returned the cheques to the bank in Cardiganshire.) As in every emergency, I sought help from my sister Anne; she was on her way to stay with a pen pal in Ardèche. I had to hitch-hike for four days to get there but I managed to do so with only the little money I still had left. (I slept the last night in a shed near Vivier cathedral and lived for days on nothing but blackberries.) It was disappointing, having reached Lablachère, to find out that Anne had been ill and was recovering at her Auntie Ruby's house in Rhiwbina.

The Rouvier family in Lablachère was extremely kind to me, and I stayed with them for a number of days, appreciating the high standard of their meals. They also lent me twenty thousand francs – a sum duly repaid by my mother. So I was able to resume my travels – to Nîmes, Marseille, Cassis (where a woman who was interested in Gladstone and had stayed in Penmaenmawr, bought me dinner) and Monaco. (The hostel in Cap d'Ail was owned by a radical organization which encouraged hostellers to make as much noise as possible in order to disturb the people who lived in the expensive houses all around.)

From Nice, I travelled through the Alps, climbing up to the hostel at St Jean; this particular lodging was eighteen hundred feet above sea level. As it was getting dark, I failed to find the hostel and slept in a telephone kiosk – an exceedingly uncomfortable experience. From there I went on to Chamonix, where I travelled on the *téléférique* to the Mer de Glace at the foot of Mont Blanc – an exciting experience. The road from Chamonix went past the Rhône Glacier (a place my mother had talked about many a time) and I went from there to Locarno and Como, and then on to Basel, Paris and Calais. My mother had sent my A level results to the youth hostel in Calais, and it was pleasing to see that they were quite promising. The British Consul in Calais had to arrange a boat ticket to get me home, an arrangement which would become increasingly familiar to me.

My greatest shock during my travels on the European continent was finding out that hardly anyone had the least inkling that such a place as Wales existed. I would talk all day with the various people who offered me lifts. As French was one of my A level subjects, I was quite fluent and I had very many conversations that went a little bit like this:

'*D'ou venez-vous?*'
'*Du Pays de Galles.*'
'*Ah, Portugal, de Lisboa?*'
'*Non, je suis Gallois.*'
'*Ah, Danois. De Copenhagen?*'
'*Non, Welsh.*'
'*Ah, Belge, de Bruxelles?*'

Every traveller from Britain was considered to be English. Indeed, there was a tendency to think that England was the home of every tourist. As the owner of a *pension* in Florence at the end of the nineteenth century put it: 'The English have arrived, but I don't yet know if the ones staying with us are Russians or Germans.' It was obvious that the people I was speaking to believed that the only nations were those which were also states. However, in Belgium and Switzerland I noticed that the language of the Coca-Cola adverts changed as I went from one linguistic region to the next. When I returned to Wales I decided that I would join any movement that strove to ensure Wales would become a state and that the language regions within Wales would all recognize Welsh in the same way as the various regional languages of Switzerland were recognized. Plaid Cymru was the only party that was interested in such matters, a party of which I have been an ardent member for almost sixty years, to the indignation and confusion of some of my relatives. There was some irony in this, as the trinity which many people see as the essentials of Welshness – Christianity, singing and rugby – did not appeal to me in the least. But surely a country that contains the Newport Transporter Bridge deserves the allegiance of every one of us?

The intention, in September 1955, was that I should apply to study English Literature at Oxford, an idea which was enthusiastically supported by Dan Jones. During the months that followed I read avidly; indeed, I do not know anyone else who has read all of Shakespeare's plays, Spenser's *Faerie Queen* in its entirety, Milton's *Paradise Lost* and Byron's long poem 'Don Juan', as well as novels such as *Clarissa* and *Pamela*. My mother would be delighted to read alongside me, and she very much enjoyed Milton's 'Areopagitica' and Byron's 'The Prisoner of Chillon'. In

January 1956, I went to Jesus College, Oxford, to sit the entrance examinations, but I wasn't successful, in part, perhaps, because I didn't sit the Latin paper, since any knowledge of the language I had once possessed had long since withered away. Looking back, I think my failure was fortunate; in the 1950s, potential students of Oxford had to do military service before going there, while in other universities this was postponed. I had no desire to 'save the Empire' and, had I joined the army, I would have taken part in that foolhardy venture, the attack on Suez. Furthermore, I agree with Roy Jenkins, who spent a year at University College, Cardiff, that the standard of lectures and care was higher in the University of Wales than in the older universities of England.

I was accepted to read English at Cardiff, an area I associated with my childhood, but there were another eight months before the start of term. Therefore, I went skiing in Scotland and afterwards cycled to London. There, I got a job paying five pounds a week, transporting cloth from a warehouse in Regent Street.

London in the 1950s was a great place, without the rush and the exorbitant prices that typify it nowadays. I paid two guineas a week for bed and breakfast in Kensington and next to nothing for food at the Welsh Club on Oxford Circus.

I also went on a bus trip to Runnymede.

'It was here,' said the guide, 'that King John sealed Magna Carta.'

'When was that?' asked an American on the bus.

'Twelve-fifteen,' came the reply.

'Pity,' said the American. 'It's twelve-thirty now, so we've just missed it!'

I went to the theatre every night, with a ticket costing anything from two shillings to see *Sailor Beware* to five shillings to go to the opera at Covent Garden. I cycled every Saturday to Kew Gardens or Hampton Court and I spent my Sundays in either the National Gallery or the British Museum.

It was a rich and pleasurable life, but my ambition lay in another direction. I wanted to go to Germany to learn German, mainly because the Germans I had met at various youth hostels the previous year had struck me as the most cultured, enlightened, multicultural and multilingual people I had ever had the pleasure to meet.

Therefore, after months in London, I cycled to Dover and travelled on to Bruges, Ghent and Brussels and then through the hills of the Ardennes to Trier. There, I saw for the first time an example of baroque architecture, a style I grew to adore, especially in light of the inspiration I derived from Monk Gibbon's book, *Western Germany* – one of the volumes I got hold of via the splendid mobile library service in Cardiganshire. It rained often, and when it did I stood under a tree and learned a poem.

I was enchanted by the Mosel valley and there, in Bernkastel, I tasted wine for the first time (I believe it was Bernkastel Doktor). The warden of the hostel in Bernkastel maintained that it was necessary to have a glass of wine before enjoying anything beautiful and refined, a point of view I have grown to agree with more and more. From Koblenz the road went up the valley of the Rhine – an enchanting journey. From there I went to Mainz and Frankfurt where, it was rumoured, there was plenty of work for everyone. But I did not have the necessary skills, and it was a real surprise to the locals that someone from Britain was looking for work in Germany. I did not manage to find any paid work to keep me in Frankfurt and, once again, the British Consul had to help me to get home, with my mother agreeing to repay the money. The Consul looked dubiously at my passport but after I had emptied my pockets in his office, I heard him say, having himself been a student at Bangor and seeing the slim volume of Welsh poetry: 'If he can read Welsh, he must be British.'

On returning to Bwlch-llan in the middle of the summer of 1956, I realized that the village had changed. We weren't connected to the water supply until the 1960s, but electricity arrived at the end of the 1950s, by which time there were houses here and there with household generators. One consequence of this was the arrival of the deep freeze, which brought to an end the customary distribution of *cig mân* among neighbours. Little use was made of the electricity supply to begin with, as villagers were afraid to commit themselves to a financial outlay they could not accurately predict. 'I like this electricity,' said one neighbour. 'It's very handy when you're coming in from milking to be able to see to find the matches to light the Tilley lamp.'

The advent of electricity transformed cattle farming, as the newfangled machines made it possible to milk a larger herd – a key to the farm expansions seen during the following decades. Almost every farmer took to selling milk through the Milk Marketing Board and their prospects changed with the arrival of a monthly cheque for their produce. Stands for milk churns were erected at the end of every farm lane, some of them with particular characteristics; originally, they were made from wood, and often the woodwork would be elaborately carved. Later on, they were built of stone and imaginatively constructed brickwork.

The arrival of electricity also allowed people to watch television, a device that quickly became very popular in rural Cardiganshire at the start of the 1960s. It revealed to them how much richer in possessions other communities were and prompted them to turn their backs on the traditional entertainments of the village. Speakers at WI lectures were very keen to teach the women of the village about such things as colour schemes, matching accessories and wall-to-wall carpeting and one of our neighbours went as far as to decorate her parlour in a 'contemporary style'. Her husband mocked her. 'You'll only be in the room for three days', he said. He was right; she was only there for three days, resting in her coffin.

There were changes, too, in the system of government payments. Mari James, from the post office in Llangeitho, claimed that farmers in the village were insisting on getting married in English.

'Why?' I asked.

'Because they want to hear the word "grant" during the service,' came the reply.

The establishment of the Farmers' Union of Wales also affected the community; it was interesting to see members of that union aligning with the Labour Party, with many, eventually, moving towards Plaid Cymru.

The greatest change was the arrival of the car, a vehicle that interested our neighbours a great deal, and I remember discussions about who owned any vehicle seen being driven through the village. There were two cars in Bwlch-llan in 1945 and some six by 1952. Neither of my parents ever owned a car, and it was not until her children bought their own cars that my mother was able to enjoy some of the splendours of mid Wales. As the general ownership of cars coincided with the advent of electricity in the area, everyone needed more money than ever before.

At the start of the 1950s families were able to boast that their only expenditure was the council rates, and many resorted to barter, bringing eggs (or, occasionally rabbits) to the shop to exchange for the things they couldn't produce at home, such as sugar, salt, tea, paraffin and yeast; not a single penny exchanged hands. It is astonishing, looking back, to realize that almost all our neighbours were self-sufficient, as they also heated their houses by burning wood or peat.

I delighted in visiting Brynhyfryd, where the sisters who lived there sustained themselves by making butter. I became adept at using both the churn and the separator, and I was very fond of buttermilk. Some of my mother's friends in Treorci thought it was much cheaper to live in the country than in the town and criticized her for not sending them a regular supply of butter. I was astonished to see how cheap butter was in Paris and brought it home as my gift from the city. It was pleasant to visit Corgam Bog where Eluned Bwlch-graig would cut peat with a special knife and then arrange for it to be taken to the Tŷ Tywarch, the peat house in the farmyard. Cold tea was poured on a peat fire so that it might smoulder until morning, when sticks were placed in it to rekindle the flames. It was alleged that the peat fire at Bwlch-graig had been alight for at least two hundred years.

I pondered about the changes occurring in my community after reading the work of the sociologist Dudley Stamp. He argued that there were three kinds of people living in the countryside; the primary people – those who were directly involved with the land; the secondary folk – teachers, shoppers, ministers and so on, who offered services to those in the primary class; and the third category – those who had an economic role somewhere else but who lived in the countryside because that was where they preferred to live ('adventitious rural dwellers'). I noticed that, during the past generation, the first category has dwindled and the second has almost disappeared, while there has been huge growth in the third category. Stamp does not mention a fourth category – people who have settled in the countryside with little intention of doing anything there.

'How are the new neighbours?' I asked someone who had some hippies as neighbours.

'Lovely,' came the reply. 'They're just the same as you or me, except that they don't work or marry.'

It has to be said that some incomers have introduced new activities into the area – pony trekking for example, along with garden centres, camping areas and luxury restaurants – and it can be argued that the countryside became more interesting as it became anglicized, although that argument holds little appeal for me.

In the Rhondda I became used to an industrial tradition which was no more than a century old, and in Cardiganshire I became immersed in a rural tradition with its roots reaching back thousands of years – a great advantage to any historian. I had ceased to live in Bwlch-llan before I fully appreciated the changes that lay on the horizon; because of them, it is now very different from the place I remember.

3

College Life

1956–63

IF THE RURAL parts of Cardiganshire were changing, then so too was my own life. During my teenage years I began to question why I had no interest in the things that interested my male contemporaries. I read (in the *Daily Mail*, I believe – a paper I have kept away from ever since) that one should be suspicious of the sexuality of any boy who didn't show any interest in sport. It was also taken for granted that all teenagers should be interested in pop music; Elvis Presley and the Beatles became very popular, but I took no notice of either of them. On the other hand, I liked the singing of Dafydd Iwan, probably because of the appeal of his patriotic messages. Such things had troubled me for years and I had begun to think that I alone was affected by this departure from the normal.

It was reassuring to read the press attention lavished on the Kinsey Report at the beginning of the 1950s – a report that suggested that a high proportion of people in their teens felt ambivalent about their sexuality. It was pleasing to be told that I wasn't the only one and that I would, eventually, grow out of it.

I decided that it would be best to ignore the whole matter and concentrate instead on those things that did interest me: gardening, walking, reading, travel and academic work. It was obvious that many other people had come to the same conclusion, judging from a report in the *Pink Paper*, a magazine that alleged that those young people ambivalent about their sexuality were more likely to succeed in examinations. I understood the desire to marry and have children but I saw no appeal in chasing after girls; with many of my contemporaries spending a good deal of time in such pursuits, I concentrated on things which were of greater interest to me. (If it becomes totally acceptable for boys to chase boys, I wonder if the situation noted in the *Pink Paper* will continue?)

When I was travelling in Germany I noticed that many men in their twenties came to the various hostels to talk to younger men, and often they would invite them out for supper. I had a lot of attention in this regard as I was, at the time, a pretty lad. ('A bit of a dish', to quote a comment made by one of my friends.) I had a vague idea of what was going on but I declined every invitation to supper. I have regretted this since because a square meal would have been very welcome to someone who was trying to travel on next to no money. Spending the equivalent of fifty pence a day was my aim while travelling.

I went to University College, Cardiff, in October 1956. I was friendly with a few girls during the three years I was there but I did not really enjoy any relationship. The saddest thing I recall during those years was going to a Hop on a Saturday night, where I saw many young ladies sitting disconsolately in rows near the wall, waiting for someone to pay them some attention. There is little doubt that one of the best innovations of recent years has been the acceptance that women can dance by themselves.

There was a substantial crew of evangelicals at the college in Cardiff – the CIFCU (Cardiff Inter-faculty Christian Union), an equivalent to the CICU (Cambridge Inter-collegiate

Christian Union) – who attempted to compete with what they saw as the unorthodoxy and liberalism of the SCM, the Student Christian Movement.

The members of the CIFCU were an odd lot. They thought we should follow the Bible and bring forth young, but when I asked how many of their children would receive divine grace, with the certainty of going to heaven, I was told only half of them. Having children in the knowledge that up to half of them would spend an eternity in hell seemed to me an appalling prospect – or perhaps I am, like the greater part of the population, theologically illiterate.

The main thing I remember about my early period at Cardiff was Emrys Roberts's fiery speech in the student debating society, condemning the assault on Suez by Britain and France. It was obvious that the old imperialist urges that I hated so much were still alive. Being an eighteen-year-old man in 1956 was a frightening experience, and the only models I had were Chris Rees and Emrys Roberts, both of whom had resisted conscription. As my political ideas had started with doubts about foreign policy and the defence of the British system, it was not sufficient to aim for a measure of autonomy. It was necessary to reject the system entirely. If that was the meaning of independence, then it should be brought forward as soon as possible. I remember a minister in the foreign office saying how happy he was that Britain was 'punching above her weight'. I suggested that what this actually meant was that we were being taxed heavily so that he could appear to be more powerful on the international stage than he deserved. He smiled sourly, but lost his seat in 1974. I became a great admirer of Emrys (who went on to become the organizer of Plaid Cymru) and under his influence I was increasingly eager to become active in the nationalist movement. I went regularly to conference and to the Plaid Cymru Summer School where I met a wealth of interesting friends, among them Meic Stephens, Harri Webb, Meic Tucker, Gareth Miles, Cynog Dafis, Peter Hourahane, John Daniel, Cennard Davies, Harri Pritchard Jones and Hywel Davies. Indeed, this was the first time I had spent time with contemporaries whose company I didn't want to leave. At college I discovered other friends as well, especially Huw Williams from Llanelli; he lives in Italy nowadays and I look forward to visiting him there.

The University of Wales insisted that students studied three subjects in the first year, and I chose English, History and Archaeology. Even though I developed a love for Anglo-Saxon literature, I did not much enjoy the English courses. But the Archaeology course was exciting; there was a wealth of treasures in the National Museum nearby and we went on digs in Dinas Powys, Penydarren and Caerleon. During the summer of 1957 I went with other members of the department to explore the remains of Hadrian's Wall.

Great revelations came during the courses in the department of History. I loved Henry Loyn's lectures about Europe in the Middle Ages and I decided that I wanted to study for a degree in History. That's how it was, and I realized that there were many more charming lecturers in the department, especially Dorothy Marshall and dear Professor Chrimes. Chrimes could come across as a little gruff (he was a near mythical figure in many History departments in Britain) but I principally remember his kindness, his interest in his students and the exhaustiveness of his knowledge. History, for him, was the constitutional growth of sovereign states, especially England, and no doubt he was dismissed as old-fashioned by more pioneering historians.

While I was a student in Cardiff I tried to travel during the holidays. I went to Ireland and Brittany, the first of many visits to these places. The trip I remember best was to the coast of Yugoslavia. I visited the island of Hvar, where lavender grew in profusion everywhere; it was possible to smell it long before the boat arrived at the harbour. A woman living in Hvar had once been a teacher in Tregaron. In the 1930s she had gone on an overseas trip arranged by the Urdd, the Welsh-language youth movement, and she later married the captain of the ship on which they had travelled; and he went on to become the harbourmaster at Hvar. They spent the years of the Second World War in abject destitution, but by the time I saw them in 1958, things had improved, not least because of the parcels sent from Tregaron. My mother arranged for her to receive a packet of needles, things that were impossible to obtain in Yugoslavia.

I became very fond of the cities of Dubrovnik and Split and I much enjoyed the train journey to Sarajevo, where there were over seventy Muslim minarets in 1958. It was interesting to note that the official language of every Putnik, or tourist office, was French; it was as if everyone had read the Versailles Agreement, a document that suggests that French is the official language of Europe. The majority of travellers there spoke German or Italian, even though the English element was growing quickly. But, somehow, French still held its own.

I returned to Dubrovnik some years later, by which time the French language had been exiled. I had supper in the company of a Frenchman who had travelled in India, south-east Asia and in America. He was extremely articulate in English. He said he was, in speaking French, aware of images associated with the language, and could almost smell them – a comment that struck a chord with me when thinking about the Welsh language. 'When I speak English,' he said, 'I feel nothing of that; it is just a thing, just a thing.' I felt that the conflicts between English and French reflected something of the tension between Cardiff and Swansea. A hundred and fifty years ago, French was the main cultural language of Europe, as Swansea was the cultural centre of Wales.

Professor Chrimes, an arch Tory, was very dubious about my visit to Yugoslavia. He was even more suspicious of my visits to Ireland. 'Nobody,' he suggested, 'should want to leave the Empire.' Nevertheless, his course on Richard III's usurpation and his enthusiastic notes at the foot of my essays were inspirational. I do not think that I shone in my finals and I suspect that he was responsible for persuading the external examiners to award me a first-class degree. Such a degree allowed me to work for my PhD at Trinity College, Cambridge, and to receive a scholarship which would support me during my doctoral studies.

After graduating from Cardiff I spent some weeks supporting Neville Williams, Plaid Cymru's candidate in West Flintshire. The north-east of Wales was entirely new to me but I am very glad that I came to know the area, as I believe it does not get its fair share of recognition in the history of Wales. (I had the same inspiration when staying, later on, at the residential Gladstone Library in Hawarden.)

From Flintshire I went on to the Plaid Cymru Summer School in Llangefni and there, outside the Black Bull, I had the pleasure of the company of some of the young intellectuals of the party. (Cynog Dafis has some interesting observations about these sessions in his autobiography, *Mab y Pregethwr* [The Son of the Preacher].) The drowning of the Tryweryn Valley was the principal subject matter of that summer school and it was arranged that we should interrupt the intended visit of the Minister for Welsh Affairs, Henry Brooke, to the National Eisteddfod in Bangor. But he was wise enough to stay away.

I also had the desire to get to know England better and hitch-hiking along the A40 became a regular occurrence. It was extremely pleasurable to visit the cathedrals at

Gloucester and Salisbury, as well as the gardens of Hidcote, and I became besotted with the Michelin tour guides. I always thought I was on the verge of arriving home when I reached Sennybridge and saw an advert for Raleigh bicycles – '*Raleigh, y beisycl sy'n ddur i gyd*' [Raleigh, the bicycle that's all steel] – almost the only Welsh advert in the whole of Wales at the time.

Meanwhile, my love for south-east Wales deepened. By changing my lodgings every term, I had the opportunity of living in twelve different parts of Cardiff and got to know the city well. The range of accommodation meant I was looked after by a legion of landladies who were keen to introduce me to a range of television programmes – especially *Come Dancing* and *Top of the Pops* – an experience that made me feel that television was not a medium which appealed to me, a feeling that has never left me. People believed that the pictures on the TV were better when viewed in darkness and so, when night fell, they would shut the curtains and sit there without any lights on. All this was strange to me as we didn't get electricity in Bwlch-llan until after I had graduated.

My sister, Anne, was teaching in Merthyr by now, and she bought a car. Every Saturday I would take the train from Cardiff to Merthyr and she would drive me to such places as the Brecon Beacons, Brecon, Tretower, Llangorse Lake, Cefn-y-Bedd, Tredegar, Ebbw Vale and Blaenavon. I did not realize at the time that getting to know Brecon and Blaenau Gwent would be so important to me. I remember hitch-hiking from Abergavenny to Merthyr. I went through Clydach – the real Clydach. There is a Clydach in the Swansea Valley and another in the Rhondda, but the real one is the one between Abergavenny and Bryn-mawr. There, I greeted two adults who were escorting children across a road. Many years later I came to the conclusion that I had met my parents-in-law, though in fact I did not meet them then, or indeed, later.

When I left Cardiff I was already dreaming about what I might do with my life. Starting a family was top of the list (two daughters and two sons was the ideal); in addition, I hoped to be able to do something worthwhile in a Welsh context, contribute to historical studies, ensure I had enough money to travel the world, own a substantial garden and learn how to write *cynghanedd*, or strict-metre poetry. Now that I am in my seventies, I think I have realized all of my ambitions – with the notable exception of the last on the list.

I went to Trinity College, Cambridge, in October 1959. There were many excellent aspects to the place – better libraries, for example – but I am surprised at the current argument that it is the duty of every secondary school in Wales to ensure that as many as possible of their pupils go to 'the best universities'. Conversation between students was richer (though it could be very old-fashioned) in Cambridge than it was in Cardiff, but there were also a great number of undistinguished people who would not have been there at all were it not for their parents' ability to pay for them to attend public schools. I met a good number of students from the north of England; they were even more confused than the Welsh cohort, who were at least a little more certain about their own identity. The subservient attitude of the inhabitants of the north of England towards those living in the south-east remains a mystery to me.

I remember a legion of able Welsh students at Cambridge, among them the brilliant mathematician Elmer Rees, Saunders Davies (who would become the Bishop of Bangor), David Davies (who became vice-chancellor of St David's University College, Lampeter), Brian Evans, a fascinating geographer from Liverpool and the computer scientist Frank Bott. I became president of the Mabinogi Society, which was hugely indebted to Alun Moelwyn Hughes, one of the few lecturers who took an interest in the activities of

Welsh students. From the student body, the one who made the deepest impression on me was Phil Williams from the Rhymney Valley. I went on a tour around Wales with him, selling the *Welsh Nation*, and during that trip I introduced Phil to Dafydd Wigley, Gwynfor Evans and Harri Webb, each one of whom acknowledged that they had just met a remarkable person. There is a tribute to Phil in *Be Nesa!* [What Next!], the fourth volume of Dafydd Wigley's autobiography, and I also wrote an article in memory of him. I like to think that I made the occasional constructive contribution to the nationalist movement, but signing Phil's application form to become a member of Plaid Cymru was the one that gave me the most pride. His death in 2003 was a national tragedy.

Much of the countryside around Cambridge was dismal. You can get an echo of the disappointment embedded in Wordsworth's line: 'I went into the fields, the level fields.' I learnt to drive there and one had to travel for miles to find land with a sufficient gradient to enable a learner to practice a hill start. But with a car at your disposal there were plenty of lovely places within reach, among them the city of Ely, the town of Thaxted, and the attractive villages of the Suffolk hills.

Among my friends at Trinity, one of the pleasantest was Richard Villebinsky, a native of Poland, whose family settled in Australia after the Second World War. He came to stay with us in Bwlch-llan. It was interesting to hear him speaking Polish with the children in the schoolyard of Ysgol Trefilan and realizing that many of them understood him. Mari James, Llangeitho, attributed the success of the bus company she ran with her husband to the presence of a number of Poles in the Aeron valley, whom they would carry to Catholic church services in Lampeter. In the middle of the 1950s there were more Polish books in the public library in Lampeter than there were Welsh-language volumes.

The students I remember best of all at Cambridge were from India. Three of them roomed with me in the luxurious house we rented on Grange Road. Mr Rasul was a surly fellow (I never discovered his first name). He was a member of a powerful family and, when Nehru came to London, Mr Rasul went to see him, in order, I imagine, to please his mother, who was a key figure in the Congress Party in Lucknow.

'What is your address?' I asked him once.

'The Mall, Lucknow,' came the answer.

'Which number?'

'Just the Mall, Lucknow,' was Mr Rasul's reply. He sat around all day complaining continually about the shallowness and greed of the Americans, and it was always a pleasure when he disappeared, though no one knew where he went.

A much more likeable character was Arun Abhyanker, who had lived in Mumbai, Rome and New York. He was the most cosmopolitan man I ever met; however, he was faithful to the Maharashtra culture – and that, perhaps, was the reason he developed a deep interest in Wales. He went on a course about Wales at the college in Bangor; I went there to meet him and we visited Llanddwyn Island, an enchanting place in his opinion. A Scot who lived in our house had a great interest in the idea of the 'Princes Street Highlander' – someone who was very proud of his connection with the Highlands but enjoyed living in Edinburgh. Arun thought the same applied to India, and he coined the term 'Rajpat Himalayan' for such a person. I felt the same was true of Wales and coined the term 'Queen Street Snowdonian'. An attempt by an Irish friend – 'O'Connell Street Macgillycuddy Reeksian' – was perhaps less successful.

My closest friend at Cambridge was Amiya Bagchi, an Economics student from Kolkata. He has, by now, gained international recognition, particularly for of his book, *The Political Economy of Underdevelopment*. He stayed with us in

Bwlch-llan on many occasions and he was delighted when the children at my mother's school referred to him as 'the black man'. I went to visit him when he was a fellow at Cambridge and Paris and I realized that he had read every book that I had ever heard of. Now that he is in his late seventies, he has grown tired of travel and it is likely that my visit to see him in 2013 will be the last. On that occasion, he gave me his latest volume, *Perilous Passage*. I arranged for him to receive a hardback copy of my book, *Hanes Cymru*. As he was very interested in what was being published in Bengali, he was delighted to show it to his friends in Kolkata; it was proof, he suggested, that it was possible to publish a richly illustrated volume in a minority language. In truth, the comparison had little substance, when one remembers that two hundred and fifty million people speak Bengali, and less than half a million speak Welsh. Yet there is one similarity, in that spoken Bengali can be very different from the written form. I had proof of that when Amiya sent me a copy of an article he had written about me for *Bangla*, one of the most important magazines in Kolkata. Not one of our Bengali friends could translate it (the language was too grand, according to them), so we had to use a specialist translating company. The article was full of praise for me and my work, although possibly Amiya over-emphasized my laziness.

This idea of that I was lazy stemmed from the fact that I would spend time in Cambridge sitting around and talking instead of frequenting the library. The sources for studying the Bute family were to be found in Aberystwyth, Cardiff, London and Edinburgh, and I was given very little guidance as I worked on them. 'Send me a postcard, if you want any help,' was my supervisor's comment. I would have received more detailed guidance had I stayed in Cardiff. In a way, I was glad that I had found my own path, as this was a help later on when I was researching other topics. The central archive, in Mount Stuart on the Isle of Bute, wasn't catalogued when I worked on the subject. I went to Mount Stuart in 2010, when the work had been carried out by the genial archivist, Andrew McLean. The archive, now fully catalogued, was so enormous that it would require at least a lifetime to go through it all; I felt that I had merely scratched the surface of the subject.

I spent many weeks researching in the National Library, staying at Dôl-y-bont with my mother, in a house she had bought after retiring as the head of Bwlch-llan school. (The house was in a parish euphoniously named Llanfihangel Genau'r Glyn – or Llanfihangel Gee Gee, as it was renamed after a scandal there involving horse meat in 2013.)

The second Marquess of Bute (1794–1848) wrote at least five letters a day; he kept copies of them all, and he also kept copies of all the replies. He did this for at least thirty years, amassing a total of more than one hundred thousand letters. The majority of them are in the National Library and I believe I have read them all. They were evidence of the diligence of a man from Scotland who wanted to revolutionize south Wales by writing letters. I worked very slowly, partly because of the nature of the material, and partly because I undertook other work at the same time.

I was standing on the steps of the National Library at the end of the winter of 1962, taking a break from the task of eviscerating the Rhondda coal leases (see the sixth chapter of *Cardiff and the Marquesses of Bute*), when Gareth Miles tried to persuade me to back his campaign for summonses in Welsh. In January, Gareth had fallen foul of the authorities over a minor offence and had sworn that, should he be taken to court, he would demand that the summons be in Welsh. When an English summons appeared in May and the magistrates refused to consider his request for a Welsh document, he spent a night in prison – the first of a long and honourable line.

Between the beginning of the case and its conclusion, Saunders Lewis delivered his radio lecture 'Tynged yr Iaith' [The Fate of the Language]. Saunders Lewis maintained that it was necessary to make it impossible 'for a government to conduct its business without the Welsh language' and he argued that this might be a basic tenet for a movement he had in mind. As he thought Plaid Cymru should be that movement, he saw no need for another. The next move was consistent with his message. In a meeting of the Plaid Cymru branch in Aberystwyth, which was held in Beti Jones's flat in North Parade (now the Eidal Fach restaurant), I suggested that the branch should put forward a motion to the Plaid Cymru conference in Pontarddulais which called on all Plaid branches to organize activities that would force the authorities to give the Welsh language official status. Tedi Millward opened the discussion and I seconded his motion. It was carried unanimously.

Neither of us wanted to see Plaid Cymru confine itself to being a militant language movement, turning its back on what Saunders Lewis called 'pointless parliamentary elections'. Both of us had great respect for Gwynfor Evans and his adherence to the ballot box, and for Emrys Roberts who was working hard to gain support for Plaid Cymru principles among those living in south-east Wales – not among the exiles from the north and west but among the indigenous folk of east Glamorgan and Gwent. These were not people who were attracted to the nationalist movement because of their anxiety about the future of the Welsh language, even though some of them grew to be very concerned about its fate.

Therefore, my invitation to those who wanted to take action to come to one of the rooms in the secondary school in

Pontarddulais to discuss further activities, was testimony to the fact that we were rejecting Saunders Lewis's strategy and aiming to establish a movement quite separate from Plaid Cymru. A dozen people gathered together – more than I had expected, and that might have been because Tedi and I were considered to be moderate. There were plenty of extremists all around us and some of those were to be very critical of us in the coming months. We were asked to arrange 'further activities, should the authorities in Aberystwyth refuse to issue summonses in Welsh'. It is impossible to receive a summons without there being an offence, so an element of law-breaking was built into our activities right from the start – accidentally, as it were.

October 1962 was a busy time. The real start of the movement was a meeting in the middle of the month in the Ceffyl Gwyn public house in Aberystwyth. There, we agreed on the name Cymdeithas yr Iaith Gymraeg, the Welsh Language Society, because of Tedi Millward's respect for the members of an earlier society with the same name which had helped secure a foothold for the Welsh language in the education system of the late nineteenth century. We entered into a prolonged correspondence with Aberystwyth's magistrates; we accepted the suggestion of Graham Hughes, a very talented member of the Law department at Aberystwyth, that plastering public buildings with posters calling for recognition for the Welsh language was the best way to proceed, and the readiness of Huw T. Edwards to serve as the society's president was very much welcomed. He contributed £5 but it was very difficult in those pre-internet days to contact supporters. Even though my mother hated the thought of her son doing anything that might result in trouble with the police, I am afraid that it was she who, via her telephone bills, largely financed such contact. I paid for the stamps used in our extensive correspondence, along with the glue and the posters (£7 13s from Aberdare Colour Printers). After our first protest, I received a cheque for two guineas from Saunders Lewis and rushed it to the bank; had I slowed down and thought for a moment, I might well have got far more than that amount for an English-only cheque signed by the man himself.

It was arranged that we should put up our posters on 2 February 1963, one of the coldest days of the twentieth century. There was no water in my mother's house, so we had to melt snow to make glue. I sent the letters inviting people to take part in the protest when I was working on the Bute archives in Cardiff and staying with Meic and Margaret Tucker in Cornwall Street, Grangetown; Owen John Thomas is in favour of erecting a blue plaque on the house. My most ardent correspondent was Robat Gruffudd (later of Y Lolfa publishers); he promised he would arrange a bus-load of Bangor students for the protest (see *Wyt Ti'n Cofio?* [Do You Remember?], Gwilym Tudur, page 24). Receiving backing from someone who had family roots in the Rhondda meant a great deal to me.

There have been many descriptions of the protest, especially on the occasion of its fiftieth anniversary in 2013. They are almost all misleading. Tedi and I had arranged to plaster buildings with posters and it was all meticulously organized. We had no intention of blocking traffic on Trefechan Bridge – a rather reckless move – and if someone had been seriously injured because of this escalation of the protest, it would have been on our consciences still. The extension of the protest was the result of the decision of the Aberystwyth police and magistrates to ignore it completely. I went with Tedi to see the police, where we urged them to arrest the protesters – without, of course, admitting that we had arranged things. Perhaps the key comment came from a *Daily Express* reporter, who said that his paper would not make any mention of the protest unless something more dramatic happened. This was overheard by some of the more hot-headed protestors and they were the ones who headed for the bridge to hold up the traffic. No doubt the protest on the bridge led to more notice from the press than sticking up posters would ever have done; if so, this was the first time in their history that the Welsh have had reason to thank that very strange publication, the *Daily Express*.

Despite the extensive publicity, the authorities remained unmoved. We wrote to every magistrates' court in Wales. Most of them promised to look into the matter, although the clerk at Brecon refused to accept a letter in Welsh. I was the first to receive a summons in Welsh, from Cardiff, due to the prompting of Ioan Bowen Rees (Cardiff Council's legal adviser at the time) and, perhaps, because of the to-do in Aberystwyth. We also wrote to all the local authorities in Wales, enquiring about the condition of ancient monuments in their care. The local authorities had previously issued a statement saying that they always answered letters in Welsh in that language. The statement was not true; interestingly, we had more Welsh replies from the English-speaking areas than from those that were Welsh-speaking. One clerk sent my letter back along with a note saying that the authority was not prepared to accept a letter unless it was in English. I arranged for a woman in Paris to send him a letter in French asking about hotels in the area. I do not know what he felt about receiving a French letter but he answered – in English, admittedly – in an entirely courteous manner.

In a meeting in Aberystwyth on 18 May 1963, we decided upon the aims of the society; a committee was formed (with John Daniel as chair) and a membership card and fee agreed. It was felt that a great many campaigns could be set in train – many more than we had the resources to sustain. Among them were the registration of births in Welsh, ensuring that electricity bills and bank cheques were in Welsh, supporting the campaigns of Bangor and Aberystwyth students to promote Welsh in those colleges and assisting Owain Owain (who ran a very lively branch in Bangor) as he strove to secure a substantial circulation for our magazine, *Tafod y Ddraig* [The Dragon's Tongue].

Our campaign against the post office garnered a great deal of attention. We arranged to seize control of a post office every Saturday and we managed to do this in Lampeter, Machynlleth and Dolgellau; the trouble that ensued after the action in Dolgellau is chronicled in Saunders Lewis's play, *Cymru Fydd* [The Wales That Will Be]. However, one of our campaigns was an abject failure. I had noticed that the names of public houses were very anglicized, as were the posters inside. I believed that their owners would change their policies if dozens of young people sat there for four hours or more drinking no more than half a pint of beer each. I arranged just such an evening, but nobody came. Nevertheless, Hancocks installed splendid plaques in all of their pubs proclaiming 'Hancocks: Arwydd Lletygarwch,' which translates as 'Hancocks: The Sign of Hospitality'. It is a campaign worth reviving.

The society's activities received the blessing of Gwynfor Evans, and it is interesting to note Emrys Roberts's comment that Cymdeithas yr Iaith has been crucial to the continuance of Plaid Cymru. But by 1963, the 1964 general election was on the horizon. As the majority of the population believed – quite correctly, perhaps – that there was hardly any difference between Plaid Cymru advocates and the protestors of Cymdeithas yr Iaith, the more institutional contingent within Plaid Cymru wanted us to moderate our actions. Perhaps I was too ready to follow their advice but I had other things to consider. My scholarship was coming to an end; it was necessary for me to look for a job and I had a great deal of work to do on my doctorate. So I withdrew from much of my political activity. But I realize now that I was, at the start of the 1960s, on the threshold of the happiest time of my life.

4

Swansea and Dryslwyn

1963–73

AT THE BEGINNING of the summer of 1963, I travelled from Cambridge to Swansea to be interviewed for a post as a lecturer in the university's department of History. It was a lectureship through the medium of Welsh, and it was offered to me. The interview itself was remarkable. It started in English under the chairmanship of Lewis Jones, a man who doubted my ability to speak Welsh as I had rather an anglicized accent at the time. The interview turned to Welsh; T. J. Morgan noticed that I had wrongly mutated some word or other and suggested I should immerse myself in his book on initial mutations and syntax, *Y Treigladau a'u Cystrawen* (1952).

I rejoiced in the fact that I would be earning a salary and would therefore have money to spend on my interests. I was living in very fortunate times, when you could be a student for six years and not accrue any debt. In addition, I could afford a three-bedroom house in Killay on the outskirts of Swansea for little more than twice my annual salary – a paradisiacal period, for sure. Following my mother's example in Treorci, I bought the freehold of the house. In the 1960s, the freehold of dwellings was a burning issue; it could be central in deciding the representation of some constituencies.

In the middle of the summer of 1963, I went with Meic

Stephens, Peter and Shelagh Hourahane and Roderic Evans on a trip right around Ireland. It was interesting to reach Skibbereen in County Cork, the place from which the Hourahane family sprang, and find out that there were more people with that surname in the Cardiff telephone directory than there were in all the Irish directories put together. I loved the landscapes of Kerry, Connemara and Donegal, and I remember the fracas in Northern Ireland when Meic Stephens told a policeman he was happy to have the opportunity to visit 'British-occupied Ireland'.

The greatest excitement awaited us in Dublin. We were at the Newport Arms in Drogheda, mainly because there was an enormous painting on the pub wall of the Newport Transporter Bridge – a construction with which I am becoming increasingly obsessed. We searched through the Dublin telephone directory looking for a cheap place to stay. As I perused its pages, I noticed that there was a telephone number for the 'President of the Republic of Ireland'. (Éamon de Valera was in post at the time.) I promptly rang the number, saying we were a group of young people from Wales; that we had a deep interest in Ireland, and it would be delightful to meet the president. His assistant invited us to tea the following day. There was something of a kerfuffle outside the palace gates when Peter leapt from the car and undressed in order to change his shirt. 'I cannot meet my president,' he said, 'in a dirty shirt.'

We enjoyed an hour of de Valera's company, and I noticed that he had an enormous clock from Newtown in his office. I asked him if he would be willing to condemn Liverpool's plans to drown the Tryweryn Valley and his answer was: 'Mr Lemass [the Prime Minister] does not allow me to talk politics any more.' As he wore a gold ring signifying that he was an Irish speaker, it wasn't strange that he should wish to discuss the Welsh language. He made many references to his visit to Caernarfon and his surprise that so many of its townspeople spoke the language. 'And it was a town,' he said; 'it was a town.' Meic Stephens wanted him to talk about his role in the Irish Civil War, but his response was to take his hearing apparatus out of his ear. He pressed a button; his assistants came into the room and we left, but not before receiving a bundle of pamphlets concerning the shameful gerrymandering of the British in Derry. (When I returned to Britain I looked in the London phone book but I could not find an entry under 'Queen of Great Britain and Northern Ireland'; there is much to say in favour of a republic.)

I settled happily in Swansea and my first cohort of students became friends for life. Without telling the department, I hired the student union's van and took them all to the court in Carmarthen, where Hywel Davies was fined for refusing to register the birth of his son in English only. It was wonderful, many years later, to hear Yvonne Matthews from Llangennech and Emyr Puw from Dinas Mawddwy saying that this was their most memorable educational experience during their time in Swansea.

I spent many a night in Merthyr, at Garth Newydd, which no longer exists. This was a busy centre for a lively crew of nationalists. Here, I came into close contact with Harri Webb, a man of broad culture, who had been immersed in the Gwenhwyseg dialect spoken by frequenters of Dowlais library, where he worked. Listening to him speak was mesmerizing and he had a decided opinion about everything. A number of people left the south-east to create a kibbutz in the south-west, and Harri's response was 'The Americans have a saying: "Go west, young man, and grow up with your country". The Welsh have a saying: "Go west, young man, and shrink with your country".' He created a great many memorable political aphorisms. When David Llywelyn, the Conservative Member of Parliament for North Cardiff,

Anne Potter (née Davies),
my mother's mother.

Anne and William Potter,
my mother's parents.

Anne and Mary Potter, my
mother and my grandmother.

My father, Daniel Davies, with his brother John in the 1920s.

My parents on the occasion of their wedding in front of Bethlehem chapel, Treorci, in 1934.

The gravestone of the Potter family in Treorci cemetery.

Our home in Dumfries Street, Treorci.

With my sister
Anne around 1940.

My parents and sister Anne
in Marcross around 1941.

With my sister Anne in our garden in Dumfries Street, Treorci.

Bwlch-llan Sunday school trip to Barmouth in 1947.

My mother and Anne in front of our house in Bwlch-llan.

The road from our house down to the middle of Bwlch-llan village.

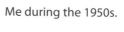
Me during the 1950s.

Pouring champagne for Hywel Teifi Edwards at the Savoy Hotel.

Our house in Dryslwyn.

Janet.

I'r Doctor John Davies ar ei ymddeoliad wedi deunaw mlynedd
fel warden Neuadd Gymraeg Pantycelyn

Lle cymysg yw prifysgol
O lawen lu a hen lol,
O haid ffêr a phraidd di-ffoedd
Ar goll tan lwch llyfrgelloedd,
O oriau pêr ar y piss
Ac abadau gwybodus.

Ger y lli, mae 'na griw llwyd –
Hen rai lyddysg difreuddwyd,
Ac yno, dro, cael aml dranc
A maeth eithafiaeth ifanc;
Yn ei syrcas, rhydd glasoed
Un naid wyllt cyn mynd i oed;
Wedi'r stŵr, mae 'na ddistâu;
Wedi'r hwyl, cadw i'r rheiliau;
Yn y bae, mae lli bywyd
Yn colli'i asbri o hyd.

Ond mae un sy'n grawd a mêr,
Un â'i wib na fynn aber,
Un ugeinoed tan scinwallt
Yn driw o hyd drwy'r dŵr hallt;
Yn rŷff cŷt, heb ei sgasff côl
Na'i fasg o hedd prifysgol;
Rhys fitnic comic yw o
A boi sydyn heb sadio;
Dau ffrydiau geiriau o'i geg:
Dilyn Rheidol ar redeg,
Haf o foi a 'bon viveur'
Tan ei growcyt yn gracyr.

Daw jîns sydd i'r warden, John,
Y denim ynysg dynion,
Y Levi's byttol ifanc,
Y brand Wrangleraidd ei branc;
Athrylith nad yw'n britho
Sy'n ei waed; Osian yw o.

Di-henaint yw y doniau,
Yn eu preim maent yn parhau:
Dawn i weld ein doeau'n nes
A dawn i gydio hanes
Y genedl ar ei gwannaf
Wrth ysbryd yr hyfryd haf.

Yr wyt sgolar 'hilarius',
Ŵr y bîb, ioga a'r bŵs;
Ŵr y geg nad yw'n or gau;
Ŵr eang dy storiau;
Ŵr ffars-owt; y sbonstiwr ffraeth;
Ŵr y dyner wardeniaeth.

Ceisiaist drwn'n ddistaw dy ddull
Dros ifanc diro sefyll;
Ein ffon a'n hamddiffynnydd
Yn y cwest mewn siambrau cudd
Ac i hurpyn ar gosped
Rhoist y gair aur, rhoist dy gred;
Y dyn mwyn – buost ein mur,
Preseli i ni'r presbylerys.

Wedi deunaw'n wardenio,
Deunaw ein tân dan un to,
Daw heno i ben deunaw bom,
Deunaw dy fynd ynom;
Deunaw o un trydan oedd
A deunaw y da winoedd.

O wahanu, dymunwn
Iti o hyd, win y tŷ hwn;
Ymhell bell eto y bo'r
Achosion dros boschuso,
'Hyd y daith, cadw dy hun
Yn haul, yn Bantycelyn.

Myrddin ap Dafydd

A verse by Myrddin ap Dafydd, presented to me by the residents when I retired as warden of Pantycelyn.

A cartoon by Tegwyn Jones, given to me when I left Pantycelyn.

My mother.

My mother's house
in Dôl-y-bont.

Janet, Conor and me in Petra's grandmother's house in Llandaff North.

The wedding of Anna and Ian at the Marine Hotel in Aberystwyth. From the left: Petra, Guto, Beca, Ian, Anna, Janet, me and Ianto.

Our children at Anna's wedding.

Beca, Trystan and me having supper at Trelluest.

Janet, Anna, Ian and
me having supper.

A photograph of me
at Gannets Bistro in
Aberystwyth.

Conor on his last year at Ysgol Gymraeg Melin Gruffydd.

Llywelyn, Iestyn and Mabon, Anna and Ian's sons.

Elin and Mared, Beca and Trystan's daughters.

Bisto, our dog and Mackenzie, our cat.

Our house in Conway Road, Pontcanna.

Walking down the avenue in my garden at Y Gors.

expressed his support for the drowning of Tryweryn, Harri commented:

David, soul of sanctity;
Llywelyn fought to make us free.
David Llywelyn, ych a fi.

Harri was no more enthusiastic about Labour supporters. When a number of Labour councillors were sentenced in court for a range of offences, Harri's response was: 'Isn't it wonderful to come across Labour councillors with real convictions?' One of the other inhabitants of Garth Newydd was another poet, Meic Stephens from Treforest, who was very supportive of Harri. We became close friends, and it was an honour for me to be asked to be his best man when he married Ruth Meredith in Tabernacl Chapel, Aberystwyth.

I went every fortnight to my mother's house to finish my work on the Bute family archive at the National Library. I would also call regularly to see Cynog and Llinos Dafis at their home, Crug yr Eryr, in Talgarreg. It was difficult to avoid talking about the activities of Cymdeithas yr Iaith when I was there, so I got fully involved again, especially in the campaign for bilingual road signs, a matter I had raised at the very first meeting in May 1963.

I had been corresponding with the clerk of Pembrokeshire County Council in the hope of persuading them to change the name of a village in north Pembrokeshire from Trevine to Tre-fin. His answer was: 'There are a number of place-names in Pembrokeshire, originally of Welsh origin, which have a well-recognized anglicized form... As long as the business of this Council is conducted in English, these forms will continue to be used.' I arranged that Meic and Margaret Tucker should measure the sign and the hooks that kept it in place, and Meic Stephens made a copy of it bearing the name Tre-fin. In the middle of a night at the beginning of

August 1964, we swapped the signs, and the English ones were exhibited in front of the Cymdeithas yr Iaith stand at the National Eisteddfod in Swansea. (See *Wyt Ti'n Cofio?*, page 31.) A policeman called by with a summons for my arrest for stealing Pembrokeshire County Council property. He was not persuaded by my argument that the Council had been given something better in exchange but, with hundreds of people standing in front of the stand, he decided it would be wiser to leave.

This was the start of the campaign for Welsh or bilingual road signs, a campaign that took all the Society's energy for at least the next five years. It was a bitter campaign and there were a great many court cases and imprisonments. The battle was won because of the diligence of Dafydd Iwan and his fellow protestors, the willingness of respectable middle-class supporters, such as Margaret Davies from Swansea and Alwyn D. Rees, to back up the protestors and the wise and far-reaching report on the issue by Roderic Bowen. I believe this was Cymdeithas yr Iaith's most important victory, as it ensured that the language was visible all over the country.

My last contribution to Cymdeithas yr Iaith was formulating, in 1964, the Society's recommendations to David Hughes Parry's committee. It had been charged with the task of explaining the Welsh language's legal status, and to consider whether changes should be made in the law. We believed that the committee had come into being as a consequence of our actions but it is just as likely that uncertainty over the validity of voting slips in Ammanford was the touchstone for its creation. We studied the status of minority – or lesser-used, a term increasingly in favour – languages, a field in which Meic Stephens was already a considerable expert. If one considers those European languages which formerly had little or no status, the safest are those which are sovereign in those areas where the majority of the population speaks the language. (For various reasons, an arrangement of this kind was not successful in the case of Irish.) We were certainly in favour of bilingual road signs throughout Wales, but we thought that any plan concerning the status of the Welsh language that was suitable for Chepstow would be much too milk-and-watery if implemented in Llanuwchllyn. It was necessary, therefore, to think in terms of linguistic regions within Wales, with different policies to reflect the distinctions between them.

The most detailed legislation on the subject is to be found in Finland. I obtained a translation of the Finnish Language Act, and this was used as the basis for our recommendations to David Hughes Parry's committee. We met the committee in November 1964 and it was clear that the chair was incensed by what he saw as 'your plan to rip Wales up'. Cymdeithas yr Iaith was the only body to suggest such a policy. Our ideas were ignored, and so the opportunity to discuss the notion that some places in Wales should have the experience of being areas where Welsh enjoyed a measure of sovereignty was lost. By the way, according to testimony released recently, civil servants in London pressed the committee to recommend very little change. Under such circumstances, it is astonishing that anything of any real value emerged from the committee's deliberations – the principle of equal validity, for example. However, it is interesting to see that Royston Jones, an acute observer, argued that there was merit in recognizing that the role and status of the Welsh language could be different in some areas from what it was in others.

At the time I was also reducing my commitment to Plaid Cymru. The last time I was present at the Executive Committee was in Aberystwyth in November 1964, when Emrys Roberts was sacked. This was a depressing incident and proof that there was no basis for the suggestion that

Gwynfor Evans was too kind to be a politician. He was, according to his biographer, Rhys Evans, the 'most absolutist of presidents'. He considered that the originality of Emrys Roberts's ideas was a threat to him and his closest friends agreed. He believed (mistakenly) that everyone from the north and the west was behind him and opposed to Emrys and that the converse was true for members from the south-east. Phil Williams's readiness to recognize how talented Emrys was greatly influenced my opinion on the matter.

Emrys had maintained for some time that he would resign as secretary of Plaid Cymru when he had a chance of another job; Gwynfor interpreted this as a resignation. The key factor was, perhaps, Emrys's divorce, and his desire to marry Margaret Tucker when she, in turn, had managed to get her divorce from Meic – a subject that attracted a good deal of attention in the popular press. If there was a light moment in the meeting, Harri Webb was responsible for it. He rose, faced the committee members and addressed them: 'Gwynfor, you dishearten me. In every meeting you complain that you get no attention in the London press, and now we are on the front page of one of the most popular Sunday papers, and you're still complaining.' Emrys lost his job but he was sufficiently gracious to stand three times as Plaid Cymru's candidate in Merthyr – and did so under the leadership of Gwynfor Evans. He worked hard, too, to ensure that Merthyr was the first council under Plaid Cymru control.

The main reason I withdrew from politics and protest was the pressure of work at the university in Swansea. The two heads of the History department, Glanmor Williams and Alun Davies, believed that a historian should be able to discuss the history of any period in any country. As a consequence, I had to peruse the excellent library extensively – an investment of time that repaid me a hundredfold later. The idea of being heads of a department in which one of the members of staff had not yet won a higher degree horrified them. I hurried to write chapters about the Bute estate, work which was praised by Glanmor Williams.

But the 1960s was a period when I had even more reason to be happy. A young woman in the department was doing research into the political history of Glamorgan at the end of the nineteenth century, under the supervision of the brilliant Kenneth O. Morgan. The university campus included plenty of places to meet and, as I spent most of the day at the college, I went to eat in the college refectory in the evening. The young woman went there too, and we started chatting regularly. The first thing that struck me was that we had been reading the same books. When referring to Levin or Natasha or Mrs Proudie, there was no need to explain anything. Her knowledge of Walter Scott was enormous – I was way behind her. If one mentioned the name Rudolph, one could almost imagine the entire Hapsburg family tree appearing on her face. She had been raised in Bryn-mawr and I think the first thing that made her interested in me was my knowledge – thanks to my sister, Anne – of Breconshire and Blaenau Gwent.

One night she brought a copy of Alun Llywelyn Williams's *Crwydro Brycheiniog* [Wandering in Breconshire] with her to supper. As she had very little grasp of Welsh, I helped her to translate it. There are many references in the book to R. T. Jenkins, and we went on to make our way through his *Ffrainc a'i Phobol* [France and its People], *Ymyl y Ddalen* [The Page's Edge] and *Casglu Ffyrdd* [Collecting Roads]. She – Janet Mackenzie Davies was her name – would read the Welsh. This was no problem as the enunciation and syntax of Welsh were both inherent in the way she spoke English. Then she would translate the content. Before long, she was totally fluent in Welsh; indeed, years later, people who met her could not believe that she had not spoken Welsh from the cradle onwards. It has to be said that the area in which she grew up was not as bereft of the Welsh language as some might imagine. There were some people in Bryn-mawr who spoke Welsh in the dialect of the area and who used lovely idioms such as: *'Mae'n dwcad y glaw'*, which translates as: 'It's pouring with rain.' In addition, D. J. Davies, Plaid Cymru's chief economist and his wife, the talented Irishwoman Noelle French – both totally fluent in Welsh – lived in Pantybeiliau, Gilwern, where they tried to establish a folk school modelled on those in Denmark.

Things had been difficult for Janet when she was young; her parents died when she was in her early teens, and she was in lodgings for a time while preparing for her A levels, before going to live with her mother's cousin, the adorable Auntie Dora, in Gilwern.

Gilwern was a village that combined the best of both the industrial and the rural cultures of the south-east, but the atmosphere of nearby market town, Abergavenny, was very different. I remember hearing a woman in the town's Waitrose saying that she was glad shops such as Tesco and Asda existed, as they ensured that ordinary people didn't go to Waitrose.

I started to look forward to supper time, when I could talk to Janet. I dreamed of spending the rest of my life in her company but I doubted whether I was qualified to be a husband. I had recently read the books of Thomas Mann and I recalled, with some horror, the heir of the Buddenbrooks family drawing a definitive line across the page under his name in the table of descent in the family Bible. Janet mentioned going elsewhere to gain a qualification suitable for a job in publishing when she had finished her thesis. I wrestled with the subject for months, but I reckoned that starting a new chapter in my life was better than losing her, and that any uncertainty would disappear with marriage.

She used to visit the National Library from time to time and it was in Cardiganshire, in 1966, in the White Lion in Tal-y-bont, that Janet agreed to marry me. By the way, she also convinced me that it was not her mother I had seen with the group of children in Clydach in the middle of the 1950s. Her mother had retired from teaching in 1941 and she would hardly have been escorting children fifteen years later.

As I had two close relatives, and she had hardly any, it was difficult to agree on the exact form of the wedding. We came to the conclusion that it would be better not to invite members of the family and married on 24 June 1966 at the City Hall, Swansea, in the presence of two witnesses, Prys Morgan and Nesta Jones – a decision that went down badly in some quarters. We then went to meet our relations in Gilwern. Janet had a great affection for the Brecon and Monmouthshire canal, so the obvious choice for a honeymoon was to hire a boat on a canal. We chose a stretch between Nottingham and Loughborough. We spent our first night in Chipping Camden and there, in memory of my first taste of wine, we had a bottle of Bernkastel Doktor, which cost twenty-eight shillings.

Even though we were on our honeymoon, we spent hours going through references to the first Marquess of Bute in the Duke of Portland Collection at Nottingham University. From there we went on to Cambridge, where we stayed with Phil and Ann Williams and took the opportunity to search out memoirs with any relevant material at the university library.

Shortly after we returned from honeymoon, the Carmarthen by-election was held on 14 July 1966 – which happened to be Bastille Day. Gwynfor Evans's victory was a matter of great joy to me, even though I have heard it argued that the result caused such a negative reaction among Welsh Labour MPs that it slowed down the move towards devolution. According to some, it would have been better if the Labour candidate, Gwilym Prys Davies, had won; his success would not have caused any backlash, while ensuring that Carmarthen had an MP who was firmly patriotic. But, as the history of Wales in the latter half of the twentieth century attests, it is impossible to speculate.

In the years after we married, I was rather heedless regarding Janet's best interests. By settling in Swansea I was denying her the opportunity of going somewhere where she could gain qualifications that would enable her to work in the world of books. There is little doubt, considering that her health was fragile, that she should not have been pregnant before her mid-twenties, and it was definitely unwise to venture to the Pyrenees in the middle of winter when she was pregnant. Nevertheless, she maintained that the trip had done her good, as she always felt better in the mountains. That must have been something to do with her upbringing in Bryn-mawr, which is over fourteen hundred feet above sea level in places.

When I returned from the Pyrenees, I was invited to take part in some radio programmes. My first attempt was presenting *O Bedwar Ban* [From Four Corners], a half-hour programme broadcast every Friday and produced by my friend, Wyre Thomas from Llangwyryfon, for the Welsh Home Service of the BBC. Each programme had a simple formula; Welsh speakers all over the world would record a piece on a cassette, saying what had attracted their attention in the place where they lived. They sent the cassettes through the post to Cardiff – an example of how primitive things were before recent technological advances – and Wyre would select and edit the material, while I would present the programme. It was pleasurable work and we had many an interesting item, not least from Catrin Nagashima in Japan. That said, it was taking valuable time that I should have been giving to my dissertation, and I had to stop the broadcasting work. Nevertheless, I made a reputation for myself as a dependable broadcaster – something that would stand me in good stead later on.

I had finished my dissertation by 1968 and I was horrified to realize that I had fashioned a treatise of over one hundred and fifty thousand words. Cambridge was not prepared to accept a research essay of over eighty thousand words. I couldn't delete whole paragraphs that I had sweated over, so it was a relief to learn that the University of Wales, at the time, had no limit on the number of words in a postgraduate thesis. I received a doctorate from that institution and the external examiners were eager to see the work published. I also penned an article about the decline of the big estates in Wales that attracted kind and favourable comment from that dear and learned scholar, Gwyn Alfred Williams.

I enjoyed living in Swansea; there were pleasant people in the department, especially Ieuan and Maisie Gwynedd Jones. I spent the afternoon when Janet was waiting to give birth at Morriston Hospital with them. I was there for the birth itself and I remember my first-born winking at me as she came out of the womb. She, according to an *englyn* penned at the time by Prys Morgan, was *'y diamwntyn mantach,'* the toothless diamond. After she had been born, I walked the main corridor of the hospital bubbling over with pride and love, feelings that have never receded for my first-born, or indeed for my other children. As both Janet and I were Davieses, we felt that the number bearing that surname should be reduced. So, as Janet had roots in Breconshire (in Welsh, Brycheiniog) we chose the surname Brychan for the eldest, Anna Heledd, and subsequently for our other children.

There were likeable people in other departments of the college, too, and through the College House arrangement we were able to meet many of them. I remember interesting conversations with Gareth Evans from the Mathematics department and J. Gwyn Griffiths from Classics. He and his wife, Kate Bosse-Griffiths, held a soirée at their home every Sunday evening and I benefited greatly from attending these, not least because they allowed me to hear the reminiscences of Dr Zaremba. He was originally a native of Poland, but he had been captured by the Soviet Army at the beginning of the Second World War. He managed to escape and walked all the way to India, pausing only to climb the occasional mountain that hadn't previously been scaled. He moved to the university in Swansea where he empathized entirely with Wales. When an orchestra from Warsaw came to play at the Brangwyn Hall, I congratulated him on his people's achievement. 'I agree,' he said. 'It is good to see us Welsh so ready to support the Poles.' He retired to Aber-ffrwd in the Rheidol Valley and he is buried there.

The stars were all in the History department. I was very fond of many of the older lecturers: Ieuan Gwynedd Jones, of course, and also Neville Masterman, Muriel Chamberlain and Elinor Breuning. I became especially appreciative of that fascinating character, Peter Stead, someone I am always very happy to encounter. Research into the history of Welsh Labour had attracted a wealth of young scholars, among them Dai Smith, Merfyn Jones, Aled Jones and Hywel Francis. Our medieval historians were renowned too, especially Ralph Griffiths, while Glanmor Williams's expert use of literary and architectural sources in his work on the history of the Church was impressive. I was favourably impressed by both the town of Swansea and its university – an effective way of provoking my son-in-law, a Sketty man, is to declare that I don't like the place. How could I not dote on a place where I met my wife and where my first-born came into the world?

But I did not wish to continue living in Killay. My ideal was to have a house with a substantial garden in a Welsh-speaking area. In 1968, I sold the house in Killay for little more than I had paid for it. (It's a shame I couldn't wait until estate agents started to boast that it was in the Olchfa catchment area – it would have multiplied the asking price.) We bought Ael-y-Bryn, a house with ten acres in Cwrt Henri, near Dryslwyn in the Tywi Valley. This was another example of my tendency to overlook Janet's best interests; her chances of having a career in Cwrt Henri were less than in Swansea, and she faced long periods of being alone, as I drove to college each day. But she says that she enjoyed many facets of life in the Tywi Valley. It was a delight to live surrounded by fields and our children loved hunting for the eggs which our hens persisted in laying in the hedges. We had delightful neighbours – Enid Ralphs and her husband, dear Colonel Ralphs, who was full of war-time stories from north Africa.

The beauty of the local area was amazing. From our house we could see Cwrt Henri mansion, Dryslwyn Castle, Paxton's Tower and the hill crowned by St Mary's Church, an interesting building which has a copy of the western arch of Strata Florida Abbey. The first part of the weekday journey to Swansea was wonderful. I would cross the river Tywi at the foot of Dryslwyn Castle and go on to Maes-y-bont, passing Golwg-y-byd – a spot that offered magnificent views of the Tywi Valley – on the way. I much enjoyed the splendid company at the Half Way public house and took advantage of the wide range of places to eat nearby. I believed that the Tywi Valley was the most beautiful place in Wales, but Janet always sang the praises of the Usk Valley and I have to admit that the view of the valley from Llanelli cemetery, where her family was buried, was stupendous. I remember Janet talking about that Llanelli, and a friend of ours confessing that he didn't know there were two places called Llanelli. 'Yes,' she said. 'The other is a miserable town in Carmarthenshire.'

When we moved to Cwrt Henri, Janet was expecting our second child. She had special care from the medical staff at Llandeilo, one of whom visited every other day to give her an iron injection. Beca was born in Llandovery hospital. There was something prophetic about the name we chose – Esyllt Rebeca Brychan – because she was to become the partner of Trystan, a splendid young man from Minffordd. We had a third child, Gruffydd Daniel Brychan (Guto) in 1972 and a fourth, Ifan Peredur Brychan (Ianto) in 1974, both born in Carmarthen. After Guto's birth I was surprised to receive many messages congratulating us on having a son; I had thought that such prejudices had long since disappeared. Guto was not very strong in his early years, but his health improved following the removal of his appendix. By now, he has climbed almost every one of the Brychan Hills – his name for those mountains in Wales which are over two thousand feet high. Although this is not as ambitious a task as climbing all the Monroes – the Scottish peaks over three thousand feet – climbing all the Brychans is still a very worthwhile achievement.

I worked hard on the land at Ael-y-Bryn, planting an extensive orchard, planning a glade of cherries and creating a rock terrace in front of the house. Then I had the idea of extending the house so that there would be a room for each of the children, with a number of bathrooms and a flat for visitors. My ambition was to have the only house in Wales with three bilingual bidets.

Work started in 1970 and within months we had spent every penny we had, including all the money Janet had inherited from her mother. This is one of the worst ways in which I ignored her needs. Our daughters spent every Saturday morning with me at Llandeilo Builders and Anna became somewhat of an expert on plumbing parts and fixtures. Some day, I thought, she will fall in love with a water engineer.

The work was completed by the middle of the 1970s; there was something atavistic about its redesigned appearance and many people saw it as a pastiche of a row of terraced houses in the Rhondda.

As we were repaying interest on interest on interest, we came perilously close to bankruptcy. However, we did manage to finish the extension and you can still see the letters J and JD above the front door. In view of the money situation, we decided that the best thing would be to sell the house and get a job elsewhere. This desire for a change of post also derived from the fact that teaching through the medium of Welsh was becoming marginalized in Swansea, such activity being increasingly centered in Aberystwyth and Bangor.

A vacancy in the department of Welsh History at Aberystwyth was advertised, a department of which dear Ieuan Gwynedd Jones was now head. I applied for the job and got it. I spent the academic year 1973/74 at my mother's house in Dôl-y-Bont and only saw Janet at weekends and during the holidays.

Our family arrangement was no longer viable, but salvation came in 1974 when Aberystwyth decided that Pantycelyn should become a mixed hall of residence for Welsh speakers, replacing the two halls (one for men and one for women) which had previously catered for them. I applied for the wardenship of Pantycelyn and got it. It would be misleading to suggest that I was merely looking for a family home; I saw many virtues in a Welsh hall of residence. I like to think that the eighteen years I spent at Pantycelyn are proof of my belief in the importance of ensuring that Welsh-speaking students have a place to live in which the Welsh language is sovereign. We moved to Pantycelyn in August 1974 and so began a brand-new chapter in our history.

5

Aberystwyth and Pantycelyn

1973–92

COMPARED TO THE department of History at University College, Swansea, we were a very small crew in Aberystwyth. Beverley and Llinos Smith looked after the Middle Ages, Brian Howells and Geraint Jenkins oversaw Early Modern Wales, Ieuan Gwynedd Jones taught nineteenth-century history and I looked after the decades thereafter. My first academic work in Aberystwyth was to prepare my essay about the Bute estate for publication. I managed to delete hundreds of paragraphs I had previously defended, and I cut the work down to a reasonable length. *Cardiff and the Marquesses of Bute* was published by the University of Wales Press in 1981; one of the main themes of the work was the wealth that accrued to the Crichton Stuart family as a consequence of their ownership of so many coal mines in the Rhondda. It was an honour for me to dedicate the book to my two grandfathers, both of whom had suffered terribly in the Rhondda coal mines. The book was very warmly received, and since the hardback version was by then on sale on Amazon for hundreds of pounds, the publishers agreed to reproduce it as a paperback in 2011. My work on the history of Cardiff and my connections with the Rhondda resulted in one of the greatest honours ever to come my way, the unveiling of the lump of coal which is the focal point of the interpretation centre at Cardiff Castle. As the Coal Exchange is now in danger of disappearing, this piece of coal is the most important symbol of the fact that Cardiff came into being as a result of the wealth that flowed from the valleys of the Taff, the Cynon, the Rhymney and the Rhondda. It is interesting to see that some of that debt is being repaid; nowadays the jobs available in Cardiff keep thousands of people in the valleys from poverty.

But before I could thoroughly settle into academic work, I had to resettle my family at Pantycelyn. Ianto moved there as a four-month-old baby. As he is now almost forty, it is somewhat embarrassing for him to be reminded by former residents of the hall of how they remember him sliding around the place on his bottom. (It's awkward for them, too, as his comments remind them how much they have aged.) Ianto went to Sussex University (the other three went to Swansea). When people reproach him with turning his back on the University of Wales, he points out that he spent eighteen years in that institution and had every right to experience another place.

I am not sure whether or not a students' hall of residence is the best place to bring up young children. There are too many people there, all attracting their attention. It is natural for children to want to follow the example of those who are older than themselves, and as not every student behaved in an exemplary manner, problems could arise. (As I prepared this volume, I thought about writing to those students who had been particularly imprudent, promising not to divulge anything about their misdemeanors as long as they sent me a substantial sum of money, but I resisted the impulse.) But we could be confident about one thing; namely that tens, if not hundreds, of people in their late teens would look after the children should they be wandering around town at night. We knew of families living in the countryside who were horrified when their children insisted on hitch-hiking into Aberystwyth on a Saturday night. This was a worry we never had to experience.

All the children went to Ysgol Gymraeg Aberystwyth and to Ysgol Penweddig. Aberystwyth sits in a glorious setting and Guto, especially, enjoyed exploring it. Janet and I went to Utrecht to buy a caravanette, and later we all went in it to France, Germany, Italy, Slovenia and Switzerland. We visited Heidelberg, where the university ran a prison for wayward students. I remember writing in their visitors' book: 'It is a pity that we do not have something like this in Aberystwyth.'

But, in truth, there were particular pleasures to be derived from living in the midst of students. I was fortunate in the geniality of people who were, and are, associated with Pantycelyn. My predecessor, Edward Ellis, was exceedingly kind, even though the establishment of a Welsh hall was not one of his priorities. In addition, I had a great deal of support from the principal, Goronwy Daniel. I was much luckier than John Llywelyn Williams at Neuadd Morris-Jones in Bangor; he received no support from his predecessor, and had to make do without much help from his principal, Charles Evans. I often spoke to John Llew; as the wardens of Welsh halls of residence we were, after all, members of the smallest trades union in the world.

The bursar, Mrs Owen, was a woman of strong character, and she was very kind to us; her deputy, Mair Nixon (née Ebenezer) was even kinder, and it is pleasing to note that a tree has been planted in her memory in Pantycelyn garden. Everyone loved Hywel Jarvis, the night porter; he was a native of Aberdare, but he lived in Corris and his concern for every one of the inhabitants of the hall was proverbial. We were also very lucky with the hall's secretaries: first Tegwen Michael from Cenarth (who spoke a lovely Dyfed dialect), then Linda Healy (a member of the folk music group, Plethyn), and in my last years, Dilys Jones, a wise, dependable woman. Some of the staff exhibited the servility that occasionally characterizes Welsh speakers. I remember talking to a woman who worked at Pantycelyn both before and after it became a Welsh-speaking hall. 'The English', she opined, 'were real gentlemen. Now we serve people who are no better than us.'

I had assistant wardens, and the one I appreciated most during my early years was Wyn James, a man from Troed-y-rhiw who had family roots in Llanddewibrefi. I never thought I would warm to an evangelical but I took to him and his wife Christine, who is, by now, the Archdruid of the Gorsedd of Bards. It was a great advantage to have an assistant like Wyn, who was tall, strong and always sober.

To many in Aberystwyth, Pantycelyn was a stronghold of racism, a home for people who believed that only those who had the pure blood of the Celts and a long Welsh lineage had the right to call themselves Welsh and live in the hall. I never felt that there was any foundation for such slanders. I believed that Pantycelyn was not intended principally for those who had spoken Welsh from the cradle but rather should provide a place for those who wanted to have a flavour of living life through the language. This meant that it was necessary to have sufficient Welsh-speaking residents to provide solid foundations. This standpoint attracted the positive support of the first of the hall's presidents during my time there – the enlightened Tweli Griffiths. I was, therefore, keen to attract Welsh learners from non-Welsh-speaking parts of the country, a policy that was central to Jac L. Williams's vision for Pantycelyn. In my early years, it was wonderful to see Jim O'Rourke from Haverfordwest (later Chief Executive of the Urdd) and Christopher Meredith from Tredegar (a prolific author in English and a considerable contributor to Welsh literature) become totally fluent in

Welsh. I became especially appreciative of a crew of students from Nelson, near Caerffili, and it was delight in 2013 to visit one of them, Derek Stockley (father of the poet, Aneirin Karadog) at his seaside home in Brittany. It was wonderful to attract students from North America, France, Germany, Malaysia and Nigeria. I was honoured to receive a Christmas card for many years from a former resident of the hall who hailed from Nigeria and who maintained that his years at Pantycelyn were the best in his life.

It was rumoured that I favoured non-Welsh speakers, and that if you came from the Rhondda it improved your chances of getting a single room. Double rooms were my greatest source of vexation and I came to the conclusion that some lines in a sonnet by Wordsworth were entirely misleading:

Nuns fret not at their convent's narrow room;
And hermits are contented with their cells;
And students with their pensive citadels.

A goodly proportion of former residents of the hall would make frequent visits. As a result, I came to accept Douglas Adams's suggestion, in his book *The Meaning of Liff*, that the word Aberystwyth is the best term for 'a nostalgic yearning which is in itself more pleasant than the thing being yearned for'.

I had my doubts about some aspects of life in the college and the town. A strong hierarchy existed in the college and I recall the wives of some professors declaring that 'Wives of junior lecturers should sit over there', while a number of the Welsh-speaking inhabitants of the town were suspicious of those who spoke the language but did not attend a chapel. I got the impression that many of the town's inhabitants despised the college and its students, although I suggested, on many occasions, that Aberystwyth, if it were bereft of the college and its associated establishments, would be less interesting in winter than even Barmouth – and it is hard to imagine a fate worse than that.

Only a few of the lecturers tried to establish friendships with students, but I felt that was precisely what I ought to do. I would invite four of the resident students to have supper with me each night and, as we would usually talk about the places from which they came, my reputation as someone who had extensive knowledge of every part of Wales grew. This belief was baseless; the truth was that I had more interest in places than in people. As I came to realize that such suppers meant that I was spending little time with my children, I gave up this convivial habit.

Instead of eating supper with students, I would talk to them over pots of tea served in the common room at ten p.m. Gwynfor Evans kept me company one evening and he was mightily pleased to see students drinking tea and playing chess before going to bed. I sometimes went to talk to students in the town's pubs, and I became a familiar figure in the Skinners, the Black Lion and the Cŵps, causing the learned Richard Wyn Jones (see *Cymru'n Gyntaf* [Wales First], page xvi) to swear that I was holding history seminars over beer. I was often quizzed about students' drinking habit, and I would always quote Anna, who had spent three years in Germany (in Essen, Emden, Kiel and Mannheim). She was of the opinion that German student drinkers matched those of Aberystwyth, but the big difference was that the German students started their drinking during a meal. 'The trouble with our arrangement', I would argue, 'is the separation of the act of eating and the act of drinking, a sad result the teetotal movement' – a comment that did not go down well in Puritan Aberystwyth. R. T. Jenkins has some insightful comments about alcohol-free restaurants, and it was in one of them that Plaid Cymru was established. Who, I wondered, managed to get Saunders Lewis into a building where he could not have a glass of wine?

Our period at Pantycelyn was the heyday of Cymdeithas yr Iaith's campaigns on issues such as road signs and television services. The most worrying period started with Gwynfor Evans's announcement in May 1980 that he was going to fast to death unless the government created a Welsh language TV channel. I was fairly sure who would be in the front rank of the ensuing battle if he carried out his intention. I had heard some of Pantycelyn's students discussing their plans, some of which were extreme. It was an overwhelming personal relief when the 'three wise men' persuaded the government to honour its original policy on the matter and to hear in September 1980 that Gwynfor Evans had given up his fast.

I did not see any evidence that language extremists were forcing other students to protest, but enemies of Pantycelyn liked to believe this. I would sometimes receive phone calls which claimed that hundreds of people wanted to see Pantycelyn close its doors. 'Give me ten names,' would be my response, and the conversation would be swiftly curtailed. Often a student would pull down a sign or climb a television transmitter in the middle of the night. Sometimes the offenders were caught by the police and their parents would call in at Pantycelyn. The protestors feared that the police would plant evidence to be used against them and therefore expected me to be present in their rooms while searches were being carried out. That's what I did, and as a result my family and I sometimes spent an entire night without sleep.

Other things also interrupted our slumbers. Residents would lose the keys to their rooms; they would then call on me to borrow the master key, but I couldn't lend it to them in case they had some mischief in mind. I had, therefore, to accompany the borrower to make sure I got the key back. This task could swallow up an hour or more's sleeping time.

Much worse were the pranksters who liked to play with the fire alarm, as that too could result in an entire night away from my bed. David Jenkins, one of the assistant wardens, had a picture of Hieronymus Bosch's vision of hell: underneath it he had written: 'Oh, no, not the fire alarm.'

I could not have dealt with all this had it not been for my assistant wardens. Indeed, it would be difficult to praise them too highly. As they were, in the main, postgraduates, they had high academic standards and, perhaps because of this, they were more knowledgeable and wiser than the majority of students. I remember our conversations fondly. I have already mentioned Wyn James; among those who followed him was the authority on the literature of the Middle Ages, Eurig Davies, the curators Dafydd Roberts and David Jenkins, the geographer Dai Rogers, the brilliant musician Lyn Davies, and his brother, the prominent historian Russell, the musician and teacher Alun Llwyd, John Rees Thomas, who now has a prominent role in the cultural life of Anglesey, the talented and capable couple Dylan and Glenda Jones, the learned lexicographer Patrick Donovan, the eisteddfod judge and expert on recitation Siân Teifi, dear Arwel 'Rocet' Jones, and the fascinating scholar, Ceridwen Lloyd Morgan.

By using their addresses, I learned where our residents came from; 25 per cent were from Dyfed, 25 per cent from Glamorgan, 20 per cent from Gwynedd, 20 per cent from the rest of Wales and 10 per cent from outside Wales – a pattern very similar to that found among students in the early years of the college. After the establishment of Ysgol Ystalyfera in the Swansea Valley, the largest cluster of residents came from the parish of Llan-giwg, the area between Pontardawe and Pontarddulais. This fact was very much welcomed by the then principal, Goronwy Daniel, who also hailed from Llan-giwg. It has been assumed that language protestors were the product of Welsh-language secondary schools, but

I got the impression that the situation was quite otherwise. Indeed, in the early years of Cymdeithas yr Iaith, almost all the members of the executive committee, except for Cynog Dafis and me, were ex-public school students.

But regardless of where they came from and wherever they had been educated, many of them were very talented. Among them was the actress Rhian Morgan, the judge Niclas Parry, a wealth of writers, including Siôn Eirian, Wiliam Owen Roberts and Bethan Gwanas, the language promoter Marc Jones, and historians Siân Rhiannon, John Graham Jones, Russell Davies and Paul O'Leary. (I was delighted that Paul succeeded me as a member of the Welsh History department.) This list is merely scratches the surface of the distinguished contributions of former inhabitants of Pantycelyn.

Welsh popular music was indebted to many groups formed at Pantycelyn and the *cerdd dant* choir was responsible, under the leadership of the talented Gareth Mitford Davies and, later, Bethan Bryn, for revolutionizing that form. (*Cerdd dant* is the singing of a counter melody to a tune played on harp.) I remember an old lady from Llanuwchllyn hitting my legs with her umbrella because she thought I was responsible for destroying the old traditions of this form of singing.

I would often organize a party to celebrate the fact that residents or former residents of the hall had won major awards in some important eisteddfod in Wales. Others became prominent in the field of politics, among them five who were elected to the National Assembly: being Carwyn Jones, Helen Mary Jones, Rhodri Glyn Thomas, Llŷr Gruffydd and Alun Davies. The only field of activity that people seemed to shun was the ministry. Considering how many ministers were trained at Aberystwyth in the early years, it is astonishing that only one of the three thousand or so residents of Pantycelyn, during my time there, became a chapel minister. Three became priests of the Church in Wales and one joined a strict Catholic order.

Wherever I went in Wales in the late 1970s I was forever meeting former residents. When I visited HTV's offices, the first thing that Elis Owen asked me was: 'Have you come to see your former students?' A crew of them had established themselves in Caernarfon, and whenever I visit the Black Boy I receive a great many invitations to drink my fill of Mŵs Piws ale. I wondered what had happened to Welsh-speaking students from Bangor, Swansea and Cardiff; it was obvious that they had not filled prominent posts in Wales.

In the 1970s there was a great deal of discussion about the possibility of establishing a nationwide Welsh-language higher education provision, Coleg Cymraeg. Its most powerful promoter was Alwyn D. Rees, the head of the Extra-Mural department in Aberystwyth and the most gifted interpreter of rural Wales. He was in favour of centralizing all lecturing through the medium of Welsh at the old 'college by the sea', the buildings that were its original home. His department stayed there, along with Education and Welsh – the most Welsh of the college's departments. There was also an attempt to ensure that Welsh-medium lectures in the department of Welsh History would be held there, a move that received a lukewarm response from students, as the vast majority of them lived up the hill at Pantycelyn.

I had noticed that the colleges of the older universities of England and the medieval colleges of other countries had evolved from halls of residence. 'Why couldn't this idea be adapted to establish the Coleg Cymraeg?' I asked, arguing that Pantycelyn would be ideal as the nucleus for such a creation. It would be possible to hold seminars and lectures on the ground floor and there was a pleasant room which could serve as a Senior Common Room. (According to Saunders

Lewis, the success of every higher education establishment springs from its Senior Common Room.) As Pantycelyn was ideally situated for visits to the National Library, college laboratories, the theatre and the Great Hall, having the Coleg Cymraeg there in the midst of the activities of the University College of Wales (the name of the establishment at the time) was better than being isolated on the margins. As the majority of the college's staff gave the proposal a rather tepid welcome, to say the least, and the most enthusiastic promoters were keen to support another scheme, nothing came of the idea – a great loss, in my opinion. That said, the announcement made in April 2014 suggests that the subject will come up again.

I was conscious by the 1980s that the students, as a body, were not the same as they used to be. I attributed the changes to two developments in particular: car ownership and the advent of central heating. In 1974 the majority of students came to college with all of their belongings in a case or rucksack. The exception was a young lady who brought two whippets to Pantycelyn with her. As some of her fellow residents walked barefoot to the bathrooms, the possibility that the whippets might have done their business in the corridor rendered the animals unpopular. I insisted that they had to leave but the owner thought my attitude towards animals in the hall inconsistent. 'Tweli Griffiths has a goldfish,' she said, and she was not convinced by the argument that there was a great deal of difference between a goldfish and two whippets.

A decade later, inhabitants were arriving at the hall in their parents' cars, the boots of the vehicles full to the brim with possessions. These belongings were then installed in bedrooms which, thanks to the central heating, were warm, a state of affairs to which the students had become accustomed at home, the idea that a whole family should sit together in front of a single fire having long disappeared. Accustomed to treating their bedrooms at home as bedsits, the students would assemble all manner of items in their rooms in Pantycelyn: a kettle and radio to begin with, then a television, a computer, a cassette player and a harp. We also used a spare room for the harps, and I remember arranging for a minister to sleep in it (on cushions on the floor) when he came to visit one of his children. When he woke to discover that he was surrounded by golden harps, he came to the conclusion that he had died in his sleep and gone to heaven!

The biggest device ever transported to a room by a student was a sun bed rather bigger than a coffin. When I protested, I was told that there was no rule banning such devices; I drew up a long list of rules but there was no way of defeating the ingenuity of residents. Having a room filled with so much equipment meant that there was little to urge one to leave it. Very few people now came to drink tea in the common room before going to bed, and we gave up the habit of supplying it. As students had their own television sets in their rooms, very few came to watch TV in the common room either. In truth, had the situation of the 1980s applied in the 1960s, it is doubtful whether Welsh halls would ever have been established, because it was the arguments about which programmes should be watched on communal televisions that gave rise to the campaign to create such halls. I felt that the decline in this kind of sociability was a consequence of the spread of Thatcherism, and that the prime minister's particular poison had affected even the radical Welsh patriots of Pantycelyn.

Pantycelyn is a stately building which was completed in 1960 according to plans drawn up by Percy Thomas – an adaptation, quite possibly, of his plan for County Hall in Carmarthen. The occasion I remember best was the visit of the Duke of Edinburgh and the Prince of Wales, when the former was relinquishing the title of Chancellor of the University to the latter. This was arranged rather furtively by the higher officials of the university, and such was the wrath of the students that they nominated Dai Francis to stand against Charles. A candidate had to be nominated by a number of members of the University's Council; when I asked Cassie Davies to sign the form, she was shocked to see that we had chosen someone as political as Dai Francis. 'Why did you not ask Gwynfor Evans?' she asked – a figure, in her opinion, who was not political at all. Nevertheless, Cassie agreed to sign the form.

The visit of the two princes to Pantycelyn was an amusing occasion, with some people circulating towards them in the hope of having a word with one of them, while others circulated the other way, to avoid having an encounter. The vote to elect the Chancellor was held in Cardiff but the result was withheld – a fact that suggests that the Prince polled fewer votes than the Welsh establishment desired. This princely visit was the only time I can recall the college authorities being eager to spend money on Pantycelyn; as a result, the place got to look a little dowdy over the passage of years. When the college decided that residents should pay for their food separately, there were demands for more kitchens in which they could cook for themselves. It was believed that cash flow from summer visitors was crucial to the financial success of places such as Pantycelyn, so the demand for en suite bathrooms became more pressing. The idea that the building was no longer fit for purpose was mooted and there was talk of closure and of relocating the students. As it happens, the loyalty of its residents to the hall is noteworthy and it is pleasing that the college authorities are now moving closer to their standpoint.

I was involved in several other projects in the 1970s and

1980s. I had the good fortune to travel, and I had special pleasure in taking Ianto to Emden and in driving to Kiel so that Anna and I could travel through Germany to Hungary, Slovenia and Italy. I had already visited Hungary, almost the only country in Europe where people are aware of Wales. This derives from the suffering of the Hungarian people under the Austrian Empire in the middle of the nineteenth century. The emperor himself visited Budapest, and it was expected that the Magyar poets should sing his praises. However, the poet János Arany wrote *A Walesi Bárdok* [The Bards of Wales], a poem based on the legend that Edward I murdered a great many Welsh poets because of their desire to defend the rights and culture of their own people. When I called at a visitors' centre and said I came from Wales, everyone who was in there started reciting *A Walesi Bárdok*. The woman in the office took a look at my passport and saw that it listed four children but no wife. (Janet had her own passport.) She decided that I was a widower and offered to marry me, not because she had taken a shine to me but because she wanted to visit Wales to see where Edward I had killed the poets. By now, there are plans afoot to establish a Gorsedd of Bards in Hungary.

Anna and I also visited Malta and we had a fascinating chat with a man who owned a restaurant in Valetta. He wanted us to congratulate him because he had arranged that English would be the language of his home.

'How will your children learn Malti?' I asked.

'They'll be able to pick that up on the street,' was the answer.

'But if everyone follows your example,' I expanded, 'there will be no children on the street to speak the language.'

He shrugged his shoulders and said, 'So what?' English was spreading quickly in Malta, even though the only words the majority of the people could say were: 'No problem.'

In 1980 I went in the company of Wyre Thomas to Israel. Flying to Athens was as much air travel as I could cope with. So we went from Athens to Haifa in a boat; we then travelled to Cairo, a journey that involved hitch-hiking through the Sinai desert and then sailing across the Suez Canal. From Alexandria we went by boat to Venice, where we caught a train home. We arrived in the splendid city of Venice on my birthday, 25 April, and I thought the band on the dockside was there to greet me; but I soon realized they were celebrating St Mark's Day. In Israel we had many interesting experiences and conversations. I recall talking to an American lady at the King David Hotel in Jerusalem.

'I understand you're travelling around this country,' she said. 'You should go to Galilee; the lake there is wonderful.'

'Much of my early education had to do with that lake,' I said.

'So you've heard about it, have you?' came her reply.

I told a waiter in Jaffa that I came from Wales. 'I know about that country,' he told me. 'That's where they hide road signs with green paint.' Our most frightening experience came on the border with Lebanon. There, we were introduced to Major Haddad, who had been doing dreadful things in the area over which he had charge. Wyre thought it might be interesting to take a photograph of me talking with Haddad. He reached into his pocket for his camera; Haddad moved quickly and in a flash had his revolver pressed against Wyre's head. Luckily, the situation was resolved without anyone getting hurt.

Another trip from which I derived a great deal of pleasure was my visit to Berlin, when the wall was an important and divisive element, lording it over everything in the city. We had to spend the night on the western side of the wall, but all the culturally interesting places were over in the east. I travelled to that sector with an American who was afraid to visit the

Evil Empire on his own. 'We will starve,' he maintained. 'Everybody knows there are no restaurants over there.' But we had a lovely supper in the Rotes Rathaus, and it tickled me to see that the prices were halved for any customers paying with a western credit card. I went a second time to the east, and it was interesting to see the rituals and documentation necessary to gain admission: the photograph (*ohne brille* – without spectacles), the precise time of the visit, a signature to confirm the number of the passport, and so on.

Berlin's museums are remarkable and I was especially fond of the Pergamon, an exciting collection of artefacts that had been transported to Germany from the Near East. It was also interesting to see volumes of Leonid Brezhnev's speeches being dusted in a shop window next door to the Soviet Union's enormous offices on the Unter den Linden. On my second visit to East Berlin, I was late returning to the border and worried that I would turn into a pumpkin should I be caught in the East after the stroke of midnight. I started talking to an Irishman and a minute before we crossed the boundary, he decided to have a pee. As the border guard thought we were together, the two of us were promptly arrested. He had a letter proving that his uncle worked for the diplomatic service and we were released immediately.

I went again to Berlin and this time visited Poland as well, including the Czestochowa pilgrimage centre. Everyone there was crawling towards the altar, and it was astonishing to see an old lady picking wallets out of the back pockets of young men in front of her. As the atmosphere was so oppressively godly, nobody said a word. I returned to Berlin and from there went on to Dresden, where I saw a performance of *Parsifal* in the city's stunning opera house. I stayed overnight in Dresden, the cause of much embarrassment when I returned to Berlin. The border officials had details of my previous visit – the bureaucrats of the East liked keeping such records – but it seems they were happy enough to get rid of me.

When I returned to Aberystwyth, I once again became very active with Plaid Cymru, and I almost won a seat on Dyfed County Council, although standing for election was a ridiculous act, as I already had four jobs. The greatest pleasure I had while working for the party was preparing a collection of articles written by Phil Williams for publication. But lecturing and researching were my main duties. I established a course on the relations between Ireland and Scotland and the British establishment. There were a good many Irish students in Aberystwyth at the time; some of them were with us at Pantycelyn and a number had been attracted by our ability to preserve the Welsh language. I went to the Pan-Celtic Festival in Killarney on many occasions. I remember sitting there talking to one of my companions from Tal-y-Bont; an Irishman came over and asked us if we spoke Welsh to each other even if there wasn't anybody else listening. In Aberystwyth, I asked one of the students from Northern Ireland which faction he belonged to; his answer was, 'I came to Aberystwyth to avoid questions like that.' I delighted in receiving postcards from Scotland written by students of mine who had been inspired by my lectures to go and visit the country.

I wrote articles about social conscience in Wales and about the mindset of Plaid Cymru leaders, but the most exciting academic invitation came on 16 October 1978. It was a call from my old friend Harri Pritchard Jones (he told me that a new Pope, John Paul II, had been elected that same day, so I am quite definite about the date). Harri was a close friend of Seán Mac Réamoinn, one of Ireland's most prominent intellectuals, who was fluent in Welsh and a member of the bardic circle, Gorsedd y Beirdd. Seán had a connection with the publishing company Penguin and they had suggested that it would be a good thing to have a history of Ireland in Irish. Apparently, the company had been harshly criticized because the volume about Canada in their series 'The History of Nations' had not given enough attention to those Canadians whose first language was not English. It was alleged that Peter Carson, the former Chief Editor of the company, had decided that the next volume in the series should not be in English.

Seán Mac Réamoinn doubted whether a volume in Irish would be commercially viable and he suggested a volume in Welsh in its place. He asked Harri to recommend the name of an author and (can I offer loud shouts of praise?) Harri put my name forward. I was invited to meet Peter Carson in London during the summer of 1979. My intention was to meet him on my return from a trip to Greece. That was a most enjoyable trip – by train from London to Paris, then to Rome and on to Brindisi; after that by boat to Corfu, before heading for Patras and Delphi. In Delphi, I asked the oracle what the fate of Wales would be but received no answer. It was a memorable experience sailing to Crete, then visiting Knossos and Phaistos and seeing the name Evans in Greek letters on a street sign. The street was named after Arthur Evans, the man who discovered the remains of the palace at Knossos and developed the idea of a Minoan civilization. The return trip through Thessalonika, Skopje, Beograd and Venice – and then on to Milan – was very interesting.

On a train in Milan someone stole my coat, which contained my money, ticket and passport. I was completely unaware of this until the train reached the Swiss border, where I was arrested on suspicion of trying to gain entry to the country without any papers. I was escorted back to Milan by armed men and had to seek the help of the British Consul once more – this time I was able to repay the British Government with my own money. The return trip was wonderful. Sydney Smith once said that his idea of heaven was 'eating pâté de foie gras to the sound of the trumpets'. My equivalent would be going on a train up the valley of the Rhine eating omelette and drinking Bernkastel Doktor – an experience I try to repeat each year.

Because of the delay in Milan, I missed my appointment with Peter Carson. Another meeting was therefore arranged later and I found him to be a delightful man. I asked him:

'Do you publish books often in languages other than English?

'Often,' he replied.

'When was the last time you published in another language?' I asked.

He went through his files and said: 'We published one for the Free French in 1940.'

'Why publish in Welsh?' I enquired.

'Because it would be a fun thing to do,' came the reply.

I had been pondering the behaviour of editors in publishing houses. They sit down and smile sweetly at you, condemning you to many, many hours of loneliness setting black marks on paper, and noting that you may or may not receive an income and praise for your work. A blank sheet of paper is what terrifies an author most, and loneliness is the most notable characteristic of his or her existence – facts of which the general public is, perhaps, unaware. But, for all that, I got the commission, as well as details of the desired length of the manuscript and a completion date, instructions that were both swiftly forgotten.

I had gone to Greece in the main to get over the great disappointment of the 1979 Referendum result. Those who are too young to remember it cannot comprehend the extent to which it demoralized Welsh patriots. Both Janet and I felt that there was no point in living in Wales any more and that we should emigrate to a place where people did believe in their country. She suggested Israel, I suggested Kurdistan, and we almost compromised on the Cotswolds. On the way back from the Penguin office, I came to the conclusion that accepting the commission had been a huge mistake. How on earth had I agreed to write a volume about Wales in a series called 'The History of Nations', when a majority of the Welsh had declared very clearly that they did not believe they were a nation? I considered writing to Peter Carson to say I was going to renege on my contract but before I sent the letter, I had a message from John Osmond saying that he was organizing a meeting on 'The National Question Again'. Without a doubt, John kept the flame burning in the 1980s, even as Thatcherism appeared triumphant everywhere. He was of the opinion that compiling a comprehensive book on the history of Wales would be of value when the devolution question was raised again, and he argued that you cannot ignore a question once it has been asked. And he was right. In 1997 a comment made by a woman in Abergavenny gave me the greatest satisfaction: 'I voted yes, because your book made Wales sound interesting.'

So I set about writing it in earnest, filling every gap in my knowledge of the country's past. And I mean every gap, even the unpublished bits of the *Episcopal Acts relating to Welsh Dioceses* and every issue of *Y Llenor* and *Welsh Outlook*. By the summer of 1982 I had ten huge volumes of notes. But I knew there was no point in trying to start writing the book while I was living in Pantycelyn, where it was my habit to sit in my office with the curtains open, in case someone called round to discuss a problem. The college was kind enough to grant me a year's sabbatical and I decided that the best place to go was the European University in Fiesole, near Florence, a place I had visited some years earlier in the company of Ned Thomas. In order to go to there I diverged from the direct route to Krakow, where I hoped to meet Lyn Davies, who was a research student in the Polish city.

As the situation in Poland was quickly deteriorating, Lyn had already left by the time I arrived, but it was interesting to hear a woman in a restaurant on the main square, the Rynek Główny, saying quite loudly: 'I think that's the warden of Pantycelyn over there.' It was Elin Wyn, a student from Bangor, who was studying Slav languages in the city. She and her family were delightful people and we travelled together to Zakopane, where there are glorious views of the mountains between Slovakia and Poland. While I was in Krakow I visited Auschwitz. The thing which affected me the most was seeing a suitcase which had belonged to a man who had been killed in the camp. On the case were labels carrying the names of Paris, Florence, Venice and Vienna, the same places as I had travelled through on my journey to southern Poland. The case also displayed the initials of its owner: J. D. I was only five years of age when the owner of the case met his end, but I felt that it was my case and that I had been killed in Auschwitz. I think this is the only time I have wept inconsolably in public.

My journey by car from Aberystwyth to Florence gave me an opportunity to visit Aachen, Rottenburg am Neckar, Trento and Bologna. In Fiesole I got down to work at once, and it was a delight to meet the students there. This establishment accepted nine students each year from every one of the countries of the European Union – that is, twenty-seven from Luxembourg, twenty-seven from the Irish Republic, twenty-seven from the United Kingdom and so on. I did not see a single Welshman or Welshwoman there. The library at the university contained hardly anything about Wales, whereas there was a plenitude of material about Ireland – another argument for establishing a Welsh state. As Florence offered better places at which to eat, as well as more museums to visit, I moved from Fiesole to the city and took up residence in the Due Fontane hotel on the Piazza della Santissima Annunziata, Florence, for ten weeks. (I also stayed at the Milton hotel in Vallombrosa, and noticed that it was sycamore leaves that filled the brooks there.) It was possible to live on next to nothing in Florence; the hotel cost seven pounds a night and I came across a restaurant that offered minestrone, spaghetti, crème caramel and half a bottle of Chianti for ten shillings (fifty pence). I aimed to write for ten hours a day, an arrangement that allowed me to see at least one Last Supper before breakfast. I memorised the arrangement of the first ten paintings at the Uffizi gallery – a feat that left a deep impression on that learned man, Professor Freud, in Aberystwyth. I would write ceaselessly throughout supper – possibly the Chianti was useful in this regard – but often I would have to spend the following morning trying to decipher the previous evening's scribbles. It was easier to write in restaurants where all of the conversation around me was in Italian, a language on which I don't have a firm grip. Sometimes groups of Americans came in; that would make things more difficult, in part because I understood what they were saying, and also because members of such an imperialist nation tended to speak very loudly. I'm sure the Britons of Caer-went whispered to each other, while the Romans of the town were considerably more audible. I discovered discos, too; because I wrote so slowly, I could ponder an extra word while waiting for the strobe lights to strike my writing paper!

I had got hold of a copy of the *Spartacus Gay Guide* – the gay encyclopaedia, as a friend of mine refers to it – and sometimes I went to a friendly bar in the Via di Colonna. No doubt the men there ogled each other, but it was the sedate nature of the place that struck me most. It reminded me of the National Eisteddfod – people of the same disposition gathering together every now and then – not that everyone has appreciated that comparison. As society in general becomes more tolerant of bisexual people, at least in Western Europe, the number of such bars is decreasing. If the majority of the people of Wales spoke the Welsh language, I think that the National Eisteddfod would suffer a similar fate.

By the middle of December 1981 I had written the first three chapters of the book, and a part of the fourth. As we had arranged that Janet and the children would spend Christmas in Italy, I drove in the direction of Rome, working on the fourth chapter in a hotel in Assisi. I wrote home every day and was glad to hear that Russell Davies, who had taken over at Pantycelyn, was a great success. The plan was to meet the family at Rome airport and go on to a villa on the Costiera Amalfitana. While looking for a villa, I went to eat at a restaurant in Ravello. A voice from a nearby table asked:

'What are you doing in Magna Graecia?'

'What are you doing?' I asked.

'I am being myself, being Gore Vidal,' was the answer.

We had a conversation about his novel, *Julian*, and he asked me about the book I was carrying. I was reading, for the third time, *Edrych yn Ôl* [Looking Back] by R. T. Jenkins.

'Who the hell is he?' asked Gore Vidal. I did not feel that offering the description 'the greatest expert on Calvinistic Methodism' would strike a chord in this company, so I said, 'A very distinguished Francophile'. 'I never did like the French,' he said, and then we started to talk about all manner of things, including his home in Ravello (he complained that the woman who kept house for him was selling the walnuts from his garden, which meant that he had to pay for the ones we ate in the restaurant), the series of novels he was planning about America in the mid-nineteenth century, and his dog, Rat, who had been in quarantine in Britain, a necessity that was at the root of his doubts about every aspect of British life. He spoke about his hopes of a career in politics and his disappointment at failing to become governor of California.

'I would have won that election had I spent another half a million dollars,' he complained.

'Could you have afforded that?' I probed.

'I am a millionaire in a small way,' he said, and went on to explain how he had been born to be the president of the United States. He frowned when I commented: 'If you want to lead your country, the least thing you should do is live in it.' He softened a little when he realized that I was the only person he'd ever met who had read his novel about Richard I. I asked him about his book, *The City and the Pillar*, and he conceded that the homoerotic content could cause problems, especially in some parts of the United States. He took me to the main hotel in Ravello, and there, to the surprise of the night porter, he pulled a great many bottles from the shelves and invited me to try any drink that took my fancy. He opened the curtains so that I could appreciate the splendid view of Minori. As I have already mentioned conversations with de Valera and Major Haddad, perhaps I should have given more attention to Vidal's last comment of the night: 'I hate name-droppers.'

Soon the family arrived at the villa I had hired in Amalfi. The place was wonderful, with a glorious view of the coast, a garden overflowing with oranges, and lizards sunbathing on the rocks. I had crossed Europe in a little Fiat but it was doubtless unwise to try to carry six people in it to the top of Vesuvius. We went to Naples, where we found that the belief that it was a chaotic city was justified, and on to Abruzzo, where we went skiing in Roccaraso.

The family returned home and I received, in Capri, the sad news that our little dog, Branwen, had died: she was the sixth girl in my life. From the Naples area, I went on to the south of Italy, to Greece and to Sicily. Even though I was travelling, I tried to write for at least six hours every day. It was thrilling to write about King Arthur in Otranto, and to see Rex Arturus immortalized in the mosaics of the cathedral floor. It was interesting to arrive in Orvieto on 22 January 1983, seven hundred years to the day that one of Edward I's clerks wrote a letter there, rejoicing that the 'old serpent Llywelyn... had been vanquished on the field of battle'. The journey through Switzerland, Germany and France was really delightful; I doted on the beautiful villages of Alsace, I mourned by the endless war graves at Verdun and I liked the landscape at Arras, one of the places which had been so prominent in the Late Middle Ages, the period about which I was writing as I neared Calais.

I had a very kind welcome on returning to Pantycelyn, with the engaging student Dyfrig Davies welcoming me back with a libation at the Cŵps. Dyfrig has enjoyed a distinguished career in television, and I like to think that I gave him a start by persuading him to appear on *Helo Bobol* [Hello People] to talk about the work of a funeral director.

I didn't stay long in Aberystwyth, because I had been accepted as a visiting fellow at the Centre for Advanced Studies in the University of Edinburgh. Part of the pleasure of being there was the learned company of Owen Dudley Edwards, a man I had already met while working on John Osmond's plans. The year 1983 was the five hundredth anniversary of the establishment of a university in Edinburgh. There was a plethora of celebrations, and the event that stands out for me was David Daiches's lecture about religion and literature in Scotland.

The family came to Edinburgh in our caravanette and we planned a tour around Scotland. While we were in Edinburgh, Janet and I had a conversation about sexuality and I got the impression that nothing I said surprised her.

When the matter became known to the children, I received nothing but support. Later on, when my sexual ambiguity received a measure of publicity, Guto was asked what he thought of it in a broadcast conversation between him and Iolo Williams. 'There are too many narrow-minded people in Wales,' was Guto's answer. 'I'm sure it's a good thing someone is shaking things up a bit.' As Ianto had been a student at Sussex University and was familiar with Brighton, nothing shocked him.

We had a grand time touring Scotland, visiting such places as Loch Ness, Culloden, John o'Groats, the gardens at Inverewe and Melrose. After we returned to Pantycelyn I realized that I had written the first six chapters of the book and had reached the second half of the eighteenth century. I counted the number of words I had already amassed, and realized that there were over a hundred thousand, thousands more than Penguin had suggested for the volume in its entirety. I had agreed that half the study would deal with the period after 1770. Therefore, it was necessary to write a further one hundred thousand words, creating a typescript that would be three times as long as that agreed with the publishers. The decision to devote half the volume to the years between 1770 and 1980 did not arise from any desire to play down the importance of earlier centuries. Indeed, I agree with J. E. Lloyd that Wales, more than almost any other country, is a country whose history cannot be appreciated without familiarizing oneself with what happened there in the Middle Ages. But having said that, one should remember that the historian, in discussing the past two centuries, is dealing with at least the same number of people as he dealt with in all the previous centuries put together. Furthermore, the majority of the subjects that interest us today have their roots in the last two centuries. Therefore, I felt that I had little choice but to write a book that was much longer than had been envisaged. In retrospect, especially when you consider the resources of today, it was difficult to write an extensive piece of prose in the 1980s. We did not have Bruce, as the Academy's Welsh Dictionary is fondly known after its compiler; there was only the first volume of the *University of Wales Dictionary*, and no internet and no word processor, which meant that it took hours just to count the words. The whole thing was written with a pen and I still have the entire manuscript. I wonder if there is some university in Texas that might want to buy it?

It was a delight being back in Pantycelyn, where I wrote most of the rest of the words. I wasn't joking when I noted in the preface to *Hanes Cymru* [A History of Wales] my indebtedness to 'the civilized society one found there which granted me both the peace and the inspiration to press on with the work'. I had finished the writing stage by the end of 1986 and I had almost a quarter of a million words. I struggled for months to reduce this number but my efforts were in vain. I would often confuse my initial mutations, or be uncertain whether 'n' or 'r' should be doubled, or if I should to use 'u' or 'i'. There was no Cysill at the time of course, so I could not check spelling and grammar online, but John Rowlands was kind enough to go through the entire manuscript and I benefited a great deal from his help.

I sent the work to the publishers in November 1987, when the inhabitants of Pantycelyn were being stirred up by TV programmes produced by Lowri Gwilym for the *Aber, Aber* series. The staff at Penguin discussed the possibility of publishing a volume three times the length they had been expecting. As it happened, the company was sufficiently understanding to agree to do this, publishing a hardback under the Allen Lane imprint instead of a Penguin softback. It was strange to hear that they were having difficulty finding an editor for a Welsh-language book.

'Where,' I inquired, 'have you been looking?'

'Everywhere in London,' came the reply.

In the end, the text was edited by staff from the Welsh Books Council and Gomer Press did the typesetting. The book was dedicated to my mother – the first of the women in my life – and it was inspiring to hear her deliver a speech, even though she was in her nineties, at the book's launch in the Old College, Aberystwyth, in late summer 1990. It is heartening to see a volume such as this being published by a company like Penguin, as it is possible to see one's work in shops right across the world. I have seen copies of the English version of *Hanes Cymru* in Auckland, Singapore, Delhi and Vancouver; there were some two dozen of them in the Twin Towers in New York and no doubt they were destroyed in the appalling attack on the building.

The volume was very warmly received, even though I felt that I had not given sufficient prominence to my belief that every historical 'fact' was dependent on its cultural context. I was incredibly proud to read Gwyn Alfred Williams's review, when he suggested he could hear an echo of R. T. Jenkins in my work. I always read some paragraphs of R. T. Jenkins before I wrote so much as a sentence in Welsh. I copied some of the stylistic features of his work, especially his love of parentheses ('I am,' he said, 'the most enthusiastic bracketer in the world.'), but I tried to distance myself from what I regarded at the time as his overemphasis on the history of religion.

The period between sending off the typescript and receiving the proofs gave me a chance to travel again and I went by train and boat to Turkey. I adored Istanbul, and it was wonderful to show the city to Janet and Anna when we visited in 2012. From Istanbul I ventured to Ankara, where I visited the world's finest collection of antiquities in the Museum of Anatolian Civilizations. I caught a bus from Ankara to

Cappadocia, and it was interesting to travel through a village called Bala, which stood on the edge of a lake, and wonder if the name was evidence of the Celtic tribe, the Galatians, to whom St Paul sent a letter. Cappadocia, with its volcanic hills and its underground cities full of Christian icons, was a mesmerising place. I stayed on the top floor of a very tall and narrow hotel. I remember standing on balconies which faced south, east, north and west and realizing that there wasn't a soul for a thousand miles in any direction who knew me. It was a wonderful feeling.

Hanes Cymru appeared a few months after I returned and I received a request for an English version of the book. This appeared in 1993, and it is interesting to note that the Welsh-language hardback version has sold more copies in the UK than the English one. The latter sold well in the United States, where it was selected as the book of the month by the History Book Club. It was surprising to me when, on a visit to the University of Berkeley in California, almost every member of the department of Celtic Studies brought me a copy to sign.

Our biggest concern in 1990 was where we would live. We had decided that we would leave Pantycelyn when the youngest of our children left secondary school, a date that was fast approaching. Janet – who still dreamed of a well-organized house – had not entirely relished the experience of living in Pantycelyn. But she had warmed to Aberystwyth, especially when she got a job in 1988 with Mercator, an organization established to study minority languages in Europe. Some of the continent's brightest and most able linguists were drawn to Aberystwyth – from the Basque country, from the Slovenian minority in Italy, from Brittany, from Scotland, from Ireland and from Friesland. As Ned Thomas, the director of Mercator in Wales, had ensured that Welsh would be the language of communication in its

Aberystwyth office, it was exciting to encounter people from all over Europe who were entirely fluent in the language. The centre also had an influence on people who were not formally connected with it. Father Fitzgerald, for example, who already had a firm command of the main European languages – ancient and contemporary – mastered Basque, and he would spend his holidays preaching and officiating at churches in the Basque country.

Our main problem was raising sufficient funds to buy a house. We had cleared the debt we had accumulated during our housing adventure in Dryslwyn but, although we had free accommodation at Pantycelyn, and the occasional cheque from the BBC and HTV, our savings were rather meagre. There were many signs that house prices were about to rise beyond what we could afford. Therefore, I decided that the best thing to do would be to give up my lectureship in order to receive an early retirement payment. This I did in October 1990, on the understanding that we could live at Pantycelyn for another two years. The idea was to stay in Aberystwyth, on the assumption that our children would want to live near their friends, and also so that we could be near my elderly mother, who was living on her own in Dôl-y-Bont. The children, however, thought that they would be more likely to meet their friends in Cardiff, where the majority of them worked. I wanted to live somewhere that did not require me to write 'SY' on any letter I sent, thereby having to declare that I was living in the vicinity of a town on the English border. But my mother's situation was paramount in my mind; my sister, Anne, was eager to help look after her but unable to do so, as she was in Sussex, where her husband was on his deathbed. I saw my mother several times a week. I took her shopping every Wednesday, I tended her extensive garden every Saturday and arranged for her to come to supper every Sunday evening. It was a matter of pride for

Guto, who had passed his driving test at the first attempt, to drive his grandmother back and forth. He would then ferry me to Brynamlwg, where I would meet my dear friends Deian Hopkin, John Williams and John Davidson; John Williams (the late John Williams, by now, alas) could produce notably barbed remarks, and it would have been wonderful to hear his opinion of Deian's knighthood.

At the end of October, round about midnight, we received a phone call from my mother – who never rang us at night – telling us that she didn't feel very well. Beca and I went to see her and promptly phoned for a doctor. He was of the opinion that she had had a small stroke, and she had many more in the hospital in Aberystwyth. Her health improved somewhat and I arranged for her to go to an excellent nursing home in Llan-non. The last time I saw her, she told me: 'If you can't do what you want to do, it's better to go tidy.' She died the following day – 21 April 1991 – on the eve of her ninety-second birthday; she was cremated, in accordance with her wishes, at Swansea Crematorium, and her ashes were scattered on the mountain above Cwm-parc. Losing both your parents is a shocking experience: you then realize that you're the next to be forgotten. I was so indebted to my mother and I still miss her. When I went away, she would ask me to phone her to say that I had arrived safely. Although more than twenty years have elapsed since we lost her, I still try to make sure that I have the means of ringing her.

With nothing to keep us any longer in Ceredigion, we bought a house in Cardiff, and no doubt we will remain in the city from now on.

6

Pontcanna and the World
1992–2000

WE HAD A tradition at Pantycelyn of arranging a dinner at the end of the summer term to honour the new graduates. In 1992 that event was supplemented by a farewell to me and my family. There were kind speeches, and I received presents from the staff of the hall – a decanter along with a bottle of fine vintage port. Arwel 'Rocet' Jones arranged also for the students of the hall to honour me. I received a cartoon, the work of Tegwyn Jones; a speech by Lyn Ebenezer; and a metrical poem composed by Myrddin ap Dafydd. I am particularly fond of one line – which referred to me as 'Preseli i ni breswylwyr' – suggesting I was like a rock, or the Preseli mountains, to the hall's inhabitants.

A good deal of work was needed on our house in Conway Road, Pontcanna, and I am extremely grateful to my successor, Gareth Edwards, for allowing us to stay at Pantycelyn until the middle of September. I remember driving to Pontcanna with three of the children (Beca had stayed in Aberystwyth, where she was working), the dog (Pryderi, the son of Branwen) and the cat (Mackenzie). It was a blessing to be able to turn the key of the door and know that no-one would be disturbing us until morning. One of the benefits of living in Conway Road was its proximity to many interesting pubs. There was substance to Lyn Ebenezer's assertion in his speech that 'the loss to The Cŵps would be the Halfway's gain.' In the Halfway I met two people who will, I hope, be lifelong friends to me. One was Meic Birtwistle; I had known him when he was a student at Aberystwyth, and it was a great pleasure to meet him regularly. The other was Jonathan Gower; the most cultured person I have ever met. My greatest sadness in the mid 1990s was the death of our lovely spaniel, Pryderi, or Bisto as I called him. I thought about rushing out to buy another dog, but felt that it might show disrespect to his memory.

Janet's work with Mercator came to an end when she moved to Cardiff but she got a job with the University of Wales Press. She developed excellent skills as a compiler of indexes and an editor of manuscripts, and there are regular requests for her expertise. While living in Aberystwyth, she had gathered material about the history of Breconshire, which was the foundation for her novel *Amser i Geisio* [A Time to Try, 1997], which has the Brecon and Abergavenny canal as its central character. The book was warmly received by reviewers and I feel that its merits should have been more widely acknowledged. As it refers to an area of Wales that is unfamiliar to the majority of Welsh speakers, perhaps an English translation would gain a larger readership. In addition, she wrote a study of the Welsh language from the standpoint of a Welsh learner brought up in a non-Welsh-speaking area, namely *The Welsh Language: A History* (new edition, with revision, 2014).

I was also writing copiously in the 1990s. I finished the translation of *Hanes Cymru* and received a request from Geraint Talfan Davies to write a history of the BBC in Wales. The work entailed long stints of research in the archives in both Cardiff and Caversham, where I amassed substantial volumes of notes. It was astonishing to see how arrogant the authorities in London had been, not just towards Wales, but also towards the English regions. (They were much more sensitive when dealing with Scotland.) I wrote the book in Lisbon, Torremolinos and in the Canary Islands. In Tenerife, I met a doctor from Denmark who took me to Loro Parque, near Puerto de la Cruz, where there was an abundance of dolphins, parrots and penguins to be seen. I heard one child in the aquarium turn to his parents and say that 'the sharks are swimming above our heads now,' in Welsh. I thought about congratulating the parents on their son's polished Welsh, but realized that Danes and Finns took it for granted that their children would speak their native languages; so I kept quiet. I went to Tenerife by train and boat, and it was delightful to return by sea to Cádiz, a fascinating city and then go by train to Seville, Madrid, Donostia and Dieppe. A ship once used to sail from Cardiff to Saint Helena via the Canary Islands, but unfortunately this service came to an end before I had the chance to make use of it.

The volume *Broadcasting and the BBC in Wales* was published in 1994. It did not delight every reviewer, although those with an interest in the inner workings of the corporation saw merit in it. Some people doubted whether a person who did not possess a television should write such a tome. My reaction was to point them in the direction of a friend of mine who is both a butcher and a vegetarian. He knows everything about preparing meat but has no desire whatsoever to eat it. After finishing the book about the BBC, I went on to prepare a volume for CADW about the Welsh landscape (*The Making of Wales*, 1996; an update and a Welsh version, 2009), a work that stirred my interest in a subject that I had formerly enjoyed, namely archaeology. As I searched for evidence right across Wales, I came to the conclusion that what we know about bygone ages is not the result of the evidence that exists. Rather, it is based on those areas we have looked at – an observation of mine that is often quoted. At the request of that original character, J. Mervyn Williams, I fashioned a volume in English and Welsh about the Celts (*The Celts*, 2000). No doubt it would have been wiser had I waited for the publication of John Koch's work, the excellent *Celtic Culture: A Historical Encyclopaedia*, before finishing these books. I was also responsible for a volume about Cardiff (2002), an essay on R. T. Jenkins and a number of articles for *Barn* and the *Western Mail*.

At the end of the 1990s, I had the opportunity to be a part of a project that was to consume many years of my life. At the request of the Welsh Academy, I agreed, along with Nigel Jenkins and Menna Baines, to edit the *Encyclopaedia*. We were fortunate to have Peredur Lynch join the team later on. Our task was essentially to produce two volumes of almost a million words each within two years. It was foolish to accept such a timetable. Indeed, Alwyn Roberts, one of the most capable figures in Welsh public life, refused to have anything to do with the scheme because of the absurdity of the deadline.

By 1999, my sister Anne and I had received our share of the money that came from the sale of my mother's house. It was enough to enable me to buy a flat in Aberystwyth. I wanted to have such a place, partly because it could be rented out in term time to supplement my pension (I would have to wait almost ten years before I could receive a state pension). I also thought that the period of the college holidays would be the best time to capitalize on the resources of the National Library while I worked on the Encyclopaedia – presuming the scheme went ahead, which it did eventually.

In the 1990s my desire to write was no greater than my desire to travel, and Janet felt the same way. She went with Anna to Berlin, Prague and Vienna; they met Karl Davies in Prague, and were amazed at his capacity to wolf down caviar. I visited Ireland on numerous occasions, and it was delightful to join the members of the Merriman Society, established to commemorate the most famous Irish-language poet of County Clare. I was also invited to address members of the Green Dragon, the Dublin Irish-Welsh Society, and discuss the Celts with Irish tourism promoters. When I was there I mentioned a comment made to me in Edinburgh, where many denied that Lothian had any connection with the Celts.

'We are Angles here,' I was told.

'Just like the English,' I answered, rather unwisely.

'Not at all,' I was told. 'When the Angles came across the North Sea, the acute Angles went north, while the obtuse Angles went south.'

We visited Scotland again when Guto and I climbed Ben Nevis, while Janet flew over the Grampian mountains and saw an osprey following the plane. It was a privilege to recite Aneirin's poetry on the walls of Edinburgh castle when I was preparing a back-to-back television programme about the Men of the North for S4C and STV, a programme that owed much to my old friend Dyfrig Davies.

Janet, Ianto and I visited Spain many times, partly to discover how Barcelona was rising to the challenge of finishing La Sagrada Família which Gaudi had started building in 1883. I went to southern Spain with Guto, visiting Seville and wandering around the Serranía de Ronda. I also went many times to France, and it was good to wander around pleasant towns like Beaune and Épernay with Janet.

I went to North America for the first time in 1995, as a result of my being invited to deliver the opening lecture at the meeting held to establish the North American Association for the Study of Welsh Culture and Society. (I wasn't their first choice, but Gwyn Alfred Williams was too ill to attend.) We flew to New York and went on to Boston, a city which enthralled me, despite spending two days throwing up – the inevitable consequence of my flying anywhere. We ate and drank with the Welsh of Cambridge, Massachusetts. We hired a car and drove across New England. The coast was stunning, but it was shocking to see, from its replica near Plymouth Rock, how small the *Mayflower* had been. The countryside was less interesting, in the main because of the decline in agriculture in the north-east of the United States. Travelling on the highways did not offer any kind of view because no one maintained the fields or attended to the hedgerows. While in New England I wrote my lecture for the Society, mainly in motel rooms.

From Boston we travelled on the train to Rio Grande in Ohio, where the meeting was being held – an area that once attracted many settlers from Cardiganshire, where there were chapels with names such as Tŷ'n Rhos. The thing that struck us most was how surprised people were when we said that we had travelled by train. Later on, I met a group of middle-aged people on a train in California who were travelling in this manner for the first time in their lives. It is remarkable to think that the United States, which came into being because of the railways, is now full of people who want to turn their backs on them.

The lecture was well received and the principal of the University of Rio Grande took us out for lunch; the campus was a teetotal area, so we had to make do with root beer, a decidedly uninteresting drink. However, the students took us to Gallipolis, on the banks of the river Ohio, where there were a number of interesting taverns. I felt awkward while being driven back, but realized that this was one of the paradoxes of teetotalism. After the conference had ended, David Krauser, a lecturer in Toronto, gave us a lift to the city of Niagara Falls, and we spent a splendid day there admiring the waterfalls. Although he was originally from the

United States, David was clearly delighted to reach Canada; as we crossed the border, his only comment was 'Adult food at last'. From Niagara, we went to Toronto, Montreal and Québec City, before heading on to Albany and New York. We wandered through Central Park, despite a warning given by a Welshwoman in Rio Grande that one should not venture there without a revolver. She took her own weapon out of her bag to show us and it wasn't difficult to believe that she was completely prepared to use it.

I went to the United States for the second time in 1997. I flew from Cardiff to Orlando, Florida, and it was fascinating to learn that the plane was going to land in Bangor. (I soon realized that this meant Bangor, Maine.) Celestial China in Orlando was interesting but the rest of the city was just a dull strip. I hired a car to visit the Everglades, where there were many huge alligators on the road. It was a delight to island-hop across the Florida Keys, if only for the many birds that dried their wings on the telegraph wires, exactly as the cormorants do on the banks of the river Taff.

From Miami I went on to Cancún in Mexico, a place that was full of Canadians on their way to Cuba. 'It's a lovely island,' one of them told me, 'because the United States government doesn't allow any of its citizens to go there.' I was enthralled by the antiquities of Mexico. I climbed up to the temple located on the top of a hill in the Maya ruins at Palenque, and felt I lacked sufficient courage to descend. I came to the conclusion that I would share the prophet Elias's experience of being fed by ravens on the top of a hill, but a couple from Switzerland were kind enough to help carry me down the stone steps. Mexico City was both enormous and truly fascinating; the national museum there is almost as good as the one in Ankara, and the home of artist Frida Kahlo was extremely attractive. I also went to the house where Trotsky was killed with an ice axe. As Mexico City is such a warm place, isn't it surprising that someone walking around with an ice axe wasn't noticed? Before he was murdered, Trotsky was reading a book bearing the title *Death Comes to the Archbishop* and the descendants of the rabbits he kept are still breeding happily.

I travelled west to see the volcano called Popocatépetl and then south to visit Oaxaca. It was terrible to see people of pre-Columbian extraction scuttling under tables in restaurants in the hope that some food would fall to the floor from the plates of diners, most of whom were of European descent. The Bishop of Oaxaca preached about the iniquities of the society in which he lived and as a result was labelled a Communist by the Mexican authorities and their allies in the United States. There were clear differences of opinion about religion in the area; indeed, in one village near Oaxaca the inhabitants worshipped Coca-Cola bottles.

I travelled from the south of the country to the north, passing through the lovely seaside town of Acapulco. My intention was to cross into the United States at Tijuana, a town chock-full of dentists, as the cost of treatment was much lower there than in California. The queues on the border were interesting; those who looked northern European were in a short, quickly moving queue, while the others were relegated to a much longer and slower one. An official told me:

'You can cross the border even more quickly when you become an American citizen.'

'Why would I want to be one of those?' I asked.

'Everyone in the world wants to be an American citizen,' came his reply.

I was on the verge of saying 'I don't' but I knew it would be unwise to argue with a border official, so I went on my way.

In San Diego I bought a ticket allowing me to travel for a fortnight on the rail system of the western US without any further payment. I went to Los Angeles, an *eccentric* city (in the true sense of the word, having no centre). It was wonderful to follow the coastline up to San Francisco. There, I received an invitation to a party in the home of the professor of Celtic Studies at the University of Berkeley and it was amazing to hear almost everyone boasting that they lived right on top of the San Andreas Fault. From San Francisco I travelled to Sacramento and then on through the mountains to Denver, Colorado. There was a descendant of one of the indigenous peoples of North America on the train, and his job was to describe his people's customs. He broke down in mid-description, saying that he was a member of a disappearing tribe which would, before long, vanish altogether. Bearing in mind the result of the 1979 Referendum, I very much hoped that I would not, in the future, have to say something similar.

I returned to San Francisco, or rather to Oakland – where there are some excellent bookshops – in order to catch the train to Vancouver. It was a splendid journey, and a memorable experience to wake up as we travelled through the Cascade mountains and the emerald forests of the American north-west. I went to visit one of the universities; there was an English Tory there, who asked:

'How much did the state contribute to the establishment of this place?'

'About forty per cent,' was the answer.

'Isn't America wonderful?' said the Tory. 'The other sixty per cent must have come from private, commercial sources.'

'No,' said our guide. 'The other sixty per cent came from the Federal Government.'

It seems likely, therefore, that many supporters of right-wing politics who go to the US completely misunderstand the mechanics of funding there.

The journey across Canada was a thrilling experience. But I felt sad arriving at Winnipeg, since my old friend,

Brian Evans, who had been a professor of Geography there, had died and would not be there to welcome me. I visited Ottawa, and it was interesting to meet a guide at the Parliament who was familiar with Wales. 'I spent a whole summer in Beddgelert,' he told me, 'building the Great Wall of China.' (He was referring, I believe, to *The Inn of the Sixth Happiness*, which was filmed there.) Halifax, Nova Scotia, was my next stop, where I followed the Bay of Fundy, the only body of water with a greater tidal range than the river Severn. I flew from Toronto to Amsterdam and from there to Cardiff, a trip which has become a favourite of mine as it means I cannot answer the oft-repeated question: 'When are you returning to England?'

There is little doubt that my most interesting journey in the 1990s was to India in 1995/6. I tried to go there across land and by boat. 'Impossible,' claimed the official at Thomas Cook. 'There are no passenger ferries passing the coast of Somalia because of the perils, and I would not recommend a client of ours to travel through Iraq, Iran and Pakistan.' It is odd how air transport has restricted our travels. (On one occasion, Beca's partner, Trystan, travelled from India to Sudan and on to Wales in a Land Rover.)

There was no option, therefore, other than to travel by plane. There were flights from Cardiff to Goa, so I went by that route. Apart from the abject poverty, I took great pleasure in everything I saw. I was in India for four months, visiting every state that was open to foreigners. Spending Christmas Eve in Kochi was fascinating; every hotel was full, so I slept in a crib in a stable. It was wonderful to travel along the canals of Kerala, to drink pot after pot of green tea in Nilgiri and to visit the most southerly part of India, where poor fishermen eked out a hard living on the shore.

Trains in India were nothing short of a revelation, and conversations with fellow travellers were extremely interesting. Although the majority of Indians took great pride in their country, I was surprised to see that many of them hankered after the British Raj, principally, I believe, because of the usefulness of the English language. I stayed in a hotel between Puducherry and Chennai and, as I ate breakfast, I thought could hear Welsh being spoken on an adjoining table. I was right, for the two people speaking were R. Gerallt Jones from the Extra-Mural department at Aberystwyth and his daughter. He organized courses at Aberystwyth for students from India and one of them joined us. He had loved his time at Aberystwyth and had learned much about modern agricultural practices there. From Chennai I progressed to Mumbai, where I visited the Nehru museum. Among the objects on display was a postcard Nehru sent from Beddgelert to his mother in Allahabad. 'You can see Snowdon from here', he informed her. As his family hailed from the astounding mountains of Kashmir, it seems odd that he was impressed by a little bump of a mountain in Wales.

From Mumbai, I went on to Delhi, where I was joined by Ianto. I am glad that my children have inherited the travel bug; Ianto was later to travel by himself around India, and the previous year Guto had visited Mexico and Guatemala. Ianto and I visited Jaisalmer – a city with remarkable architecture – and then rode across the Thar Wilderness on the backs of camels, a very painful experience. We went from Jaisalmer to Varanasi, and Ianto was dispirited to see it getting dark for the second time during our journey. We had not booked rooms and were astonished by the readiness of Indian soldiers to offer us their beds – it is hard to imagine British soldiers doing the same for Indian visitors.

The trip from Varanasi train station was exciting. We travelled by auto-rickshaw – a mode of transport of which I was becoming increasingly fond. We had to negotiate the

Great Trunk Road; the traffic congestion was appalling, but our driver somehow managed to weave his way forwards. Varanasi was remarkable. We sat on the ghat watching bodies being burned as our heads were massaged. We visited Bodh Gaya, where it is said the Buddha had his spiritual awakening (Bodhimandala), and where every Buddhist country has erected a lavish temple. From Varanasi we travelled by bus to Nepal. We stayed in a hotel whose owner averred that his father ate a whole goat every week. We climbed a hill to get a better view of Annapurna; as Ianto, with his customary courtesy, had learned some elementary Nepali, he greeted everyone we met on the road in that language. Someone asked me: 'Why does your son speak such beautiful Nepali?'

By now, Ianto had tired of trains and buses, and he insisted we flew to Delhi. The plane journey followed the crest of the Himalayas and offered stupendous views. From Delhi we went to Agra and saw the glory of the Taj Mahal, a World Heritage Site. One should remember, however, that it is a grave; I was delighted when Blaenavon was given the same status, since it is a place where something started – the industrial revolution – rather than a symbol of the end of someone's life. After we had returned to Delhi, we went to see a *son et lumière* show in the city. It was very cold; when Ianto saw me stuffing copies of the *Times of India* under my clothes (paper is excellent insulation), he pretended not to know me. He flew home to Wales, and as it was a long and tiring journey, he fell asleep on the bus and woke up in Sarn services; Janet had to fetch him from there.

After he had left, I realized that I had not seen anything of the north-east and north-west of India, so I went to Fatehpur Sikri and Simla, and then on the wonderful train journey from there to Amritsar. It was very pleasant to go to the foot of the Himalayas at Manali and on to Jammu; unfortunately it was impossible to visit the famous town of Srinagar, with its wealth of residential houseboats.

My main reason for visiting India was to see Kolkata, as I had heard so much about the place from my friend Amiya in Cambridge. As it turned out, he wasn't there, but I found the place very much to my liking, if only for the opportunity it gave of appreciating the true significance of crowds. The memorial to Lewis Pugh of Aber-mad in the cathedral there is interesting: 'His body was returned to the land of his fathers, to Llanbadarn Fawr in Wales.' I went from Kolkata on the splendid train that takes you to Darjeeling, where I found accommodation at the Planters' Club. I had my own fire and buckets of coal and the servants were dressed as maharajas. It was interesting to visit the library to see what sort of books were read there by members in its heyday. It was obvious that the favourites were the novels of Warwick Deeping. By the way, when I visited Berlin, I noticed that he was also the favourite author of the Kaiser's family; it's odd how one generation's preference can be forgotten by the next.

From Darjeeling I went to Sikkim, where I met a member of the government of Bhutan who was taking his son to one of the Eton-like public schools that are dotted across India's mountainous regions. He wanted me to visit his son's school, as he did not believe a single pupil had met what he described as an 'Englishman from birth'. Feeling that it was not a correct description of me, I did not go. He invited me to visit Bhutan, but when I realized that it was necessary to exchange a significant sum in dollars daily during the visit, I declined the invitation. I have since regretted this, as very few Welsh-speaking Welsh people have visited Thimphu.

After I had returned to Kolkata, I visited the cemetery where Thomas Jones, the Calvinistic Methodist missionary to the Khasi Hills, is buried. I had read about his life story in Nigel Jenkins's excellent book, *Gwalia in Khasia*. Nigel described the problems he faced in trying to visit the Khasi Hills but I knew that, in the mid-1990s, the area was open to foreigners. I travelled there, using Nigel's book as a guide. In Shillong I found out that the book was being serialized in a local newspaper and I went to see the editor. 'Do you know', he asked, 'that your archdruid is in town?' I visited the Polo Towers hotel and there I had breakfast with Dafydd Rowlands, T. James Jones and Tegwyn Jones. I also went to Cherrapunji, the wettest place on earth, so it is said. I saw the grave of Freddie Bach, the son of a missionary; I took tea and watched the waterfalls that flow down the hills to the flatlands of Bangladesh. 'Dry season rain', observed the waiter. It is little wonder that Nigel, in his splendid prose, noted: 'Pincered between the lethal surges of the Bay of Bengal and the annual deluge of monsoon water, much of it draining off the Khasi Hills, these coastal Bangladeshis are seasoned precisians of life's murderous whimsicality.'

I returned to Delhi and headed for home. After the crowds of Kolkata, it was strange to be back on the half-empty streets of Cardiff, and I still hope to revisit India. But I had work to do; I was hoping to do a little broadcasting, if only to make some money to pay for my travels. I appeared on many programmes in the 1990s, and the one that gave me the most pleasure was commenting on the results of the 1997 Referendum. I had been in Scotland the previous week, where a positive result was expected. I somehow doubted that the same would be true in Wales and the early results were very disappointing. But that astute commentator Vaughan Roderick warned us that it was far too early to come to any definite conclusion. I had presented many a programme directed by his father, Selwyn, a lovely man. He had also been a supply teacher at Bryn-mawr Primary School and was delighted when Janet – his favourite pupil, according to him – repeated comments he had made about the significance of the Welsh language.

But back to the programme. The tensions of referendum night were enough to shake one to the core, but I noticed that the 'Yes' vote was increasing as the results arrived from Welsh-speaking areas, Labour-voting areas and areas where the majority of the inhabitants had been born in Wales. It is interesting to see that the 'Yes' vote was higher in Blaenau Gwent (54.6 per cent) than it was in Anglesey (50.9 per cent). The three significant factors noted above were strongly present in Carmarthenshire. I thought to myself that the matter would probably be settled by the vote there, and that there would be a nice symmetry to the story, in that it was Gwynfor Evans's victory in the Carmarthen by-election of 1966 that put devolution on the agenda in the first place. When the final result was announced, I cried in front of the cameras with joy, but misquoted Wordsworth: 'Bliss is it at this morn to be alive, but to be middle-aged is very heaven.' I stressed the middle-aged, as they could remember the disappointment of 1979 and knew that another chance would be unlikely to come in their lifetime. I walked home from Llandaff to Pontcanna as day broke; and a new dawn was truly breaking. Nevertheless, it was amusing to hear a French commentator expressing his surprise that the Scots had to make do with a *parlement*, while the Welsh, a people less confident about their independence than the Scots, in his opinion, were honoured with an *assemblée*.

By 1998 it looked likely that the team that had already been named would have to carry the burden of creating the Encyclopaedia. I felt it would be a good idea, before the work started, to go on a long plane journey, in case my loathing of aeroplanes eventually put me off flying for ever. In 1999 I decided to fly around the world, but before I could put my ticket to use the news broke about Ron Davies. Everyone was talking about it and I heard a lot of malicious gossip. I doubt whether such conversations would have taken place had the subject been racism or anti-Semitism, but it was clear that many people thought it acceptable to be disparaging about people who were sexually ambivalent. I felt that I should say: 'Listen, you are talking about me and my kind.' But I kept quiet until I was asked by *Barn* [Opinion] magazine to write an article about contemporary Welsh politics. This was the opportunity, I thought, for me to reveal the truth about myself. As Ron Davies, the main hero of devolution, was being stigmatized, I thought it would be a good thing to remind people that not everyone who was bisexual wallowed in lechery, as Vicar Prichard put it. I wrote an article on the subject and received an invitation to be interviewed on television by Tweli Griffiths. Janet was in favour of the article, as every word was carefully considered, but she thought there was something too unpredictable about a TV interview. I did not watch the programme as I had, by then, used my ticket and landed in Washington D.C.

I greatly enjoyed Washington but I came to the conclusion that the centre of the city was not as attractive as the centre of Cardiff. I had every opportunity to visit the Capitol, the White House and the Supreme Court without being asked for any documents – this was before 2001. I went to Chicago, a decidedly unfriendly city, even though it was interesting to see the painting *American Gothic* by Grant Wood and to appreciate the fruits of the earliest phase of modernist architecture.

As I had already seen Niagara Falls, the Florida Keys, the Everglades and the Cascades, I was eager to see the chief wonder of the American landscape – the Grand Canyon. I did not fully comprehend the distance between Illinois and Arizona and I felt that I had been travelling for ages through incredibly dull countryside as the train made its way from Chicago to Flagstaff. The Grand Canyon was spectacular, especially under snow. We were told that it would be warmer at the bottom of the canyon but that it would be dangerous to try to get there by way of the frozen steps, so I was content to admire the astonishing view from the canyon's edge. I went on to Los Angeles, where I stopped at an internet café. It was clear that people had managed to get hold of my e-mail address and there were many messages, written in response to my article. One suggested I should turn to Christ, while two said they were willing to remain friends with me as long as I admitted I had strayed from the straight and narrow. (Admission is an irrelevant word in this context; you admit to a crime, but you recognize a condition.) The majority of the messages were full of gratitude, proof positive that my comments had given hope and confidence to many of my compatriots, something of which I am very proud.

From Los Angeles I crossed the equator at night – the best time to fly – and landed in Auckland. I doted on New Zealand. Everyone was exceedingly welcoming but there was evidence of the inhabitants' love of rugby everywhere, with the Red Dragon flying above every camp and engravings of the Millennium Stadium on the windows of bus stations. When it was discovered that I was a Welshman who had no interest whatsoever in rugby, the comment I tended to hear was: 'But you must be a member of a male voice choir.' When I revealed that I had no interest in singing, I was told: 'I didn't think there was anything else.' 'Yes', I would answer, 'there is; we have the Newport Transporter Bridge.' I stayed on a farm near Dunedin for a few nights; the owner spent every December (our June, as it were) shearing in Wales, and it was strange to discuss farm names in the Tregaron area with him.

On Christmas night I was on Stewart Island, to the south of South Island, and it was wonderful to sit outside the hotel in sunshine at half past ten at night. I returned to South Island and visited Christchurch, a charming place, parts of which have, alas, been damaged by an earthquake. There I met a farmer, and I stayed with him on his farm on Canterbury Plains; I also had the opportunity to see whales near the coast. Then I crossed over to North Island and flew from Auckland to Melbourne, where the Welsh church is a centrepiece in the city. I visited Sydney too, and there I studied the list of those transported in a museum exhibit about emigration. It was a shock to see that a large proportion of them were called John Davies. The Australians were very friendly but when I was in Canberra on Australia Day, I saw another aspect to the character of some of them. A group of descendants of the indigenous people was protesting in front of the Parliament, and a number of men of European extraction were shouting at them: 'Go home, you black bastards.'

I travelled to northern Queensland, where I saw a tropical rainforest for the first time. Cairns is a beautiful place (that was where it was announced that Blaenavon was to be a World Heritage Site), and the town stands at the foot of Mount Bartle Frere, named after an imperialist from Gilwern. From Cairns, I went to see the Great Barrier Reef, which is without doubt one of the great wonders of the world. On the way back, the boat ran through a group of salties (salt-water crocodiles) and they had a pretty surly look about them. On an eco-tour, our guide managed to locate a duck-billed platypus, which is certainly a very odd-looking animal, as well as an emu, an extraordinary bird.

The journey between Queensland and Alice Springs is lengthy, but it was interesting to see the red heart of Australia and venture through its many canyons. I sympathized with the tadpoles, which had been born in pools that were sure to dry up in the midday heat. From Alice Springs I went to Adelaide on the Ghan railway, so called because it was built with the assistance of camels imported from Afghanistan. Indeed, one can see the descendants of the original camels through the carriage windows of the train. It is a slow journey, but it used to be even slower. It is said that a heavily pregnant woman tried to persuade the driver to get to Adelaide more quickly, as she was about to give birth. He replied: 'You shouldn't catch the train when you're pregnant.' 'I wasn't pregnant when I caught it', she retorted.

One of my fellow travellers was a student who was learning Malay. He was totally convinced that the only future for Australia was to recognize that its inhabitants lived in a country in south-east Asia and that they should stop pining for the empire. He was firmly in favour of the republican movement, which had the catchy slogan, 'Resident for a President'. A referendum was held, but as the population received no assurances that they would decide who was to be president, it was unsuccessful; however, it is interesting to note that a recent prime minister – a woman originally from Barry – has expressed a desire to resurrect the issue.

From Adelaide I went on the train to Perth. The journey seemed to last forever; the view was the same at nightfall and daybreak, as the railway went in a straight line for mile after mile. The travellers had the opportunity to go round the gold mines at Kalgoorlie, and it was interesting to see that the company owning the mines was called the Sons of Gwalia. In Perth, I went up the Swan river to visit some of the vineyards of Western Australia, and it was delightful to watch kangaroos prancing along the riverbank. It was also possible to travel down the river to Fremantle, where the Cappuccino Strip was extremely luxurious.

I flew from Perth to Singapore – a strange state, in my opinion. The place I liked the most was the café where people brought their caged canaries every Sunday morning so that they could sing to each other. The atmosphere in Singapore was oppressive and everything was very neat and clean; luckily, the Indian neighbourhood was delightfully messy. I much enjoyed travelling by bus to Kuala Lumpur and then on to Thailand. In Phuket, I experienced something quite unfamiliar to me, a pang of Puritanism; perhaps I should have such a feeling more often. I returned to Kuala Lumpur and flew from there to Amsterdam and thence on to Cardiff. This was the first time I had enjoyed a flight. I started at daybreak and the sun shone all day. There were no clouds and flying over India, Arabia, Sudan and Egypt and seeing the world pass below, was thrilling. We crossed the Black Sea, where the ice of winter still had the Crimea in its grip. The Australians on board expressed wonder at the proximity of European cities to each other. It was good to return to Pontcanna after being away for four months.

Soon after my return, Janet mentioned how much she had enjoyed having the house to herself for such a long time and said she would like this to be a permanent arrangement. Her words didn't surprise me, as she had often said that she would like a house of her own and the means to maintain one. Living by myself was acceptable to me too. As I set a plate of chocolate by my bedside to watch the little mice climb up to eat it – a spectacle that delights me every night – it is little wonder that nobody wants to share a house with me. So we set about making sure that we had a house each. We had been talking for a while about selling the house in Conway Road. Now that the children had left, we didn't need five bedrooms, and it would be better for us to be free of the mortgage.

While we waited to sell our house, we found a house for Janet in Grangetown. Bruce Griffiths uses the word 'maenor' for grange in the Welsh dictionary he compiled, and that is also the form used by Cardiff Council. The grange in question was a temporary building on the western side of the Taff estuary, a farm belonging to, but very remote from, Margam Abbey, where the abbey's servants spent part of the year tending the animals that grazed on the marshes. There were a number of temporary dwellings on the hills of Cardiganshire, and these were called *'lluestai'* or granges. So, Trelluest is the Welsh name I chose for Grangetown and it is good to see that it is being adopted and used by Welsh speakers. Grangetown is divided into two by Corporation Road; the eastern part belonged to the Bute estate and the streets bear the names of collieries – Ystrad, Aber, Bargoed and so on. The western part belonged to the St Fagans estate and many streets are named after estate farms, such as Pentre-baen and Rhydlafar. Janet was delighted that her house was on Clydach Street, even though this commemorates a colliery in the Rhondda, and not the real Clydach, near which she grew up.

We believed that there would be enough profit from the house in Conway Road for me to buy a house in Grangetown as well. It was interesting to find that more Welsh speakers came to view our house in Pontcanna than had come to see our house in Dryslwyn when that was put on the market. While the Conway Road house was for sale, I moved to the flat in Aberystwyth. The house sold quickly and before I had bought something in Grangetown, I saw an advert for a smallholding in Dyffryn Paith, near Aberystwyth, less than a mile from the place where my grandfather had worked on a farm more than a century earlier. Gors Uchaf is rather an austere place; there is electricity, but only one bedroom; the rates are £96 a month, but there is no dependable road leading up to the house, and no mains water or sewerage. But it is surrounded by five acres of land and therefore satisfied my desire to own a large garden. Another advantage was that Tafarn y Gors, otherwise the New Cross Inn, was just a field away and had a good reputation for its food. The smallholding had belonged to an English couple, self-styled hippies Mr and Mrs Page, for eighteen years. I felt that Mrs Page yearned for more creature comforts but Mr Page had wanted to stay there; he stressed that he had planted sufficient trees around the house to keep them in firewood for the rest of their days. I doubted whether I should buy a second house in the countryside but, since Gors Uchaf had been on the market for two years and was unsuitable as a family home, my worries evaporated. I bought it and Janet came with me to meet Mr and Mrs Page on the first day of the twenty-first century. I was well over sixty years of age, and embarking on a new adventure.

7

Y Gors and Grangetown

The Early Years
of the Twenty-first Century

THE MAIN DELIGHT of the early years of the twenty-first century was having grandchildren. The first to become a father was Guto. I used to think that mountain climbing was his greatest delight (he has succeeded in climbing nearly all the Brychans), but his main interest is, in fact, popular music – an interest that, quite frankly, I do not share. Guto is now the manager of Clwb Ifor Bach in Cardiff and he also has responsibilities at Maes B, the young people's zone at the National Eisteddfod. He became friendly with Petra – who, just like his mother, has roots in Blaenau Gwent. Although her health was extremely fragile, Petra was eager to have a child and a son was born to them on 2 March 2003. He, Conor Isak, is the eldest of my grandchildren; he is by now eleven years of age and has started his first year at Ysgol Uwchradd Glantaf. He is incredibly lovable and his interests are very agreeable to me. He delights in old things and takes great interest in animals. He amassed a collection of sheep skulls and has given it to me.

The next to have a child was Anna. She began doing research into German literature but made the mistake of choosing an author who was still alive. She was halfway through mastering the topic when her subject wrote several more books. She worked at the Royal College of Art in Kensington and then for Plaid Cymru, before becoming chief executive of the National Association of Head Teachers in Wales. At the moment, her job entails working to improve the levels of literacy and numeracy in Wales. While she was with Plaid Cymru, she got to know Ian Titherington who had stood as a Plaid candidate in Swansea West. A water engineer, he is responsible for Cardiff's drainage systems, and I had been right to predict, all those years ago in Dryslwyn, that Anna would fall in love with a water engineer. Ian comes from Sketty; his forebears on his father's side came from Liverpool and his mother had roots in Treorci. Indeed, she was one of the Davieses of Dumfries Street, but there is no evidence that she belonged to our Davies clan. Ian is the great-nephew of Donald Davies, the scientist who ensured that computers could connect with one another; it was a real pleasure to accompany him to Treorci to unveil a blue plaque to his great-uncle. Anna and Ian were married at the Marine Hotel in Aberystwyth in November 2002 and spent their honeymoon in Cuba. They have three sons: Mabon Brychan Titherington (2005), Llywelyn Brychan Mackenzie Titherington (2008) and Iestyn Brychan Josua Titherington (2010). I dote on them all and it is wonderful to see them at their home in Grangetown. It appears that Mabon and Llywelyn's chief delight is following football clubs in the English Premier League, although I have convinced myself that the attraction lies in the mathematical basis of the scoring. That said, Mabon has displayed talents as a poet, while Llywelyn seems adept at art. I heard that Anna was expecting Iestyn when Janet and I were having dinner in a restaurant in a snowy Ravenna. He is now four years of age and I have high hopes for him.

After an assortment of jobs, Beca went to train as a teacher and she is now head of History at Ysgol Uwchradd Dyffryn Conwy. She lives with Trystan Llwyd Evans in a delightful house overlooking the castle in Caernarfon; a home with a fine view. Trystan is a surveyor with the Eryri Housing Association and he and Beca have two daughters, Elin Llwyd Brychan (2008) and Mared Llwyd Brychan (2010). I dote on my granddaughters and one of life's greatest pleasures is going to Caernarfon to see them and their parents. It saddens me that I cannot see them more regularly but they are always very welcoming when I do have a chance to visit. They have a caravan and enjoy spending time in Aberdaron, where Conor, too, has a whale of a time.

Ianto works for Literature Wales and there are no signs of impending fatherhood. His partner, the talented broadcaster Yvonne Evans, is a great fan of rugby, while Ianto delights in football; his favourite team is Crystal Palace, which happens to be the name of the pub he used to frequent in Aberystwyth. I very much hope that disagreements over sport do not mar their happy relationship.

There have been many other pleasures. It was an honour to be given the white robe of the Bardic Circle, Gorsedd y Beirdd, at the National Eisteddfod; being appointed an Honorary Professor at Aberystwyth University; winning the Glyndŵr Prize at the Machynlleth Festival; being elected a member of the Learned Society of Wales; becoming an Honorary Fellow of the Coleg Cymraeg Cenedlaethol; and winning the Welsh Academy's Wales Book of the Year award for *Hanes Cymru* and Literature Wales's Wales Book of the Year award for *Cymru: Y 100 Lle i'w Gweld Cyn Marw* [Wales: 100 Places to See Before You Die]. On a more frivolous note, I enjoyed winning a competition in the *New Statesman*. I sent in a cutting taken from a magazine by way of a response to a column called 'This England', a title which I did not warm to, as the *New Statesman* claimed to be a magazine for the whole of Britain. The comment came from *Exchange and Mart* in 1964: 'Titled lady selling a billy goat; election of Labour government sole reason for sale.' Members of the royal family could be just as reactionary. George V was so surprised to receive a radical message from Lloyd George that he wrote the word 'Balls' on the edge of the page. It was an inelegant word in the view of his secretary, so he changed it to 'Round Objects'. The king received a message from Lloyd George asking: 'Who is Round, and why does he object?'

Reading the previous paragraph, I realize that I have certainly reached my anecdotage; so I should stop, and before long I shall do so.

As Janet, Anna and her sons, Guto and his son and Ianto all lived in Cardiff, I heard regularly about all the family goings-on. As a consequence, I began to feel isolated in Aberystwyth, so I sold the flat there and bought a house in Grangetown. This had its disadvantages, as I could no longer slip over to garden at Y Gors for an hour or two when the sun was shining. It was also dismal to lose contact with Gannets, that splendid restaurant. In addition, I missed the companionship of the Cŵps, especially the interesting chats with the brainy Richard Wyn Jones and my relative, Gareth Lewis. Brendan and Glynis Somers at the Cŵps were very kind to me, and when they got into difficulties I was only too happy to help. That said, I came to the conclusion that the wisest comment uttered by one of Shakespeare's characters was made by Polonius.

But these are minor losses when compared with the pleasure of being back among the family. Most of the children and grandchildren live within a short walk of my house, and living near Grange Gardens gives me an opportunity to get to know Grangetown and its people a little better. I have become increasingly fond of this suburb. There is a saying in the English midlands which suggests that people who have failed in life go 'from clogs to clogs in one generation'; the same, perhaps, might be said of someone who was born in a terraced house and is likely to die in one. If so, then I have been a failure, as the house I now own is exactly the same size as the house where I was brought up in Treorci. I have friends from the Taff Valley who boast that their houses in north Cardiff are much grander than the places in which they were raised, but I view this with disdain. It is much better to live in Grangetown than in Pen-y-lan. Ian and I are frequent visitors to the Cornwall tavern and the welcome in Merola's restaurant is almost as good as the one in Gannets. Clarence Hardware is the best hardware shop in Wales and the existence of the barrage keeps us all safe from flooding. For those of advanced years, there is much to be said for living in a flat area; indeed, in a decade, when I am the owner of a Zimmer frame, I shall consider it nothing short of paradise. It is also pleasant to be able to use my free bus pass to get to Cardiff Bay or the city centre.

The main attraction of Grangetown is the variety of people who live here. Indeed, you can see the whole world within a square mile. When the area developed in the second half of the nineteenth century, it was mainly an Irish area, evidenced by the number of Catholic churches and schools. In the twentieth century it became home to Somalis, Pakistanis, Iraqis, Indians and people from the Caribbean and from Africa. The Somalis are a strong local community; a book has been written about them and, according to a Radio 4 programme, everybody in Muqdisho is familiar with the name Cardiff. On the same programme, there were comments by a Somali who was teaching Welsh to other Somalis, and I once spoke to a woman with roots in Maharashtra who wanted to be a 'Welsh lady'. I like my son-in-law's habit of following the American style and speaking of 'Italian Americans' and 'Muslim Americans', rather than the British style and talking about 'British Italians' and 'British Muslims'. The noun should always take precedence over the adjective, giving us 'Italian Welsh' and 'Muslim Welsh'.

And if we have Iraqis and we do in Grangetown – then why not Cymracis? That's the term I once heard a neighbour of ours use when Janet and I were speaking Welsh in Grangetown. A great number of Welsh-speaking young people have moved into the area and it is good to see their peaceful co-existence with their various neighbours. These neighbours know they will never be the dominant element in Grangetown and the same applies to the Welsh speakers – and this might be the key to happily living side by side. I believe that the Welsh-speaking Welsh in Grangetown are entirely happy to live with immigrants from Eastern Europe, south Asia and Africa. But they are dubious about those who embrace the ideas of UKIP – people who believe that the English should run things in all parts of the United Kingdom. However, we should remember that Grangetown was the location for the first Welsh-medium school in Cardiff and that the demand for Welsh-language education is growing there daily.

While I was in Aberystwyth and then in Cardiff at the turn of the millennium, my main task was working on the Encyclopaedia. The timetable required us to finish the two enormous volumes by 2001. It was believed that our inability to stick to the deadline resulted from indolence on our part, or meant that we were choosing to do other things instead of concentrating on the Encyclopaedia. The timetable assumed that every article we received was ready for publication when we received it and that our main task was simply to arrange the articles alphabetically. This was a false assumption. We got the occasional polished contribution but many, if not most of them, had to be rewritten. But we persevered. The difficulties were especially apparent in the case of the Welsh-language volume and it was only the unstinting commitment of Menna Baines and Peredur Lynch that ensured the Welsh version was at least as good as the English one.

Nigel Jenkins was equally steadfast in his labours on what he referred to as *Psycho*. It was nothing short of wonderful to see him polishing rough sentences sent in by contributors and turning them into burnished prose. Nigel and I would exchange at least half a dozen e-mails a day, and it was with deep sorrow that I attended his funeral in February 2014, when he died at the early age of sixty-four. He had talents similar to those of Harri Webb, who was also raised in the Gower countryside. When he attacked George Thomas, Viscount Tonypandy, who delighted in his role as Speaker of the House of Commons, he penned the amusing line: 'May his garters garrotte him.'

The entries on communities were my special responsibility. Contributors were asked to write about every community in the counties for which they were responsible, but they tended to write copiously about areas they knew well and more or less ignore the rest. I had to write hundreds of entries from scratch. Although these communities had been in existence in Wales since the reorganization of local government in 1974, many contributors were entirely unaware of them and wrote nothing but nonsense.

We were answerable to Peter Finch at the Academy and to Ashley Drake at the University of Wales Press. As I was also suffering at the time from the comments of Paul Starling in that rag called the *Welsh Daily Mirror*, I once suggested in a meeting that we were oppressed by 'too many birds'. The only thing I will say is that we tolerated Drake and Finch, and I'm sure they would say the same about Nigel, Menna, Peredur and myself. A threat was made that the Encyclopaedia would be published without being edited and I, along with others, had to protest vociferously against this. Some people argued that everyone whose achievements were worthy of an article in the Encyclopaedia would have made their contribution by the time they were sixty years of age and that, therefore, we should include entries on people who were still alive. We believed that older people were capable of astonishing things and we were right – Gwynfor Evans was almost seventy when he threatened to fast to death unless a Welsh-language TV channel was established. Therefore we decided, in the end, that it would be wiser to measure a person's contribution after he or she was dead.

Throughout 2003 and 2004, we were so busy with the Encyclopaedia that I was beginning to forget to do things such as eat and sleep. There were signs that we might finish everything by 2005 but we had to deal with an external editor who knew next to nothing about Wales. He tried to insist that we should record that the rugby team in Llanelli played at Parc Howard rather than at Stradey Park. He was also responsible for the photographs, and it was interesting to see that he was keen to include a picture of the prom at Llandudno, South Africa. To accompany the article about lifeboats, he chose an image of one in Dorset. When I complained about this, his answer was, 'No one will notice.' But my son-in-law had already noticed and we had great help from his father – who spends his retirement as a coastguard on Gower – in securing an image of a lifeboat based in Wales. As we thought we should draw attention to people and places that did not have their own entries, we decided that we needed an index. The one we were offered was appalling and so we had to set about compiling new ones in Welsh and English; it was a particularly laborious task and without Janet's help we would never have finished the job.

By 2006, the typescript was with the press and I felt we could take a break. But while the two volumes were being prepared for publication, Penguin asked if anything interesting had happened in Wales since they received the typescript of *Hanes Cymru* back in 1986. I said that quite a few things had happened in the country between 1986 and 2006 and received a request to update both the Welsh- and the English-language volumes. I am grateful to Dewi Morris Jones from the Books Council for his help with the update. The two volumes were published in 2007 and it is good to see that they sell well.

The two volumes of the *Welsh Academy Encyclopaedia of Wales* appeared in 2008 and I came to the conclusion that book reviewing in Wales is rather unsatisfactory. Other than the comments of Tegwyn Jones and Jan Morris, hardly any reviews were worthy of attention. Very few reviewers had read our notes in the foreword, so few of them understood our guidelines with respect to communities, or on entries on people who were still alive. We realized that the contents of the Encyclopaedia had already dated even before publication, but so far nothing has come of any plans to update it.

By the time I had finished work on the Encyclopaedia, writing had become a burden, and I desired nothing more than a rest. However, I had promised Y Lolfa a volume about the places in Wales people should see before they die. This was published in 2009, with an English version the following year. Then I did take a break, and I wrote hardly anything until I started work on this little volume in January 2014. I worked on it until the middle of February – roughly a week for every decade of my life. I am surprised, when I look back at years that strike me as being particularly busy, that I do not have more to say.

During the post-Encyclopaedia years, my main activities were finishing the design of the garden at Y Gors, travelling, and doing some lecturing and broadcasting. The work at Y Gors proceeded apace but I came to realize, as I passed the seventy-year mark, that I was not as quick as I used to be. Ian and Trystan were kind enough to come along to help me clear the place and cut trees. I am responsible for a grove of beech trees, a circle of cherry trees and gardens full of heather and azaleas. I planted hundreds of daffodils, snowdrops and bluebells, and I started work on an ambitious water garden. Unfortunately, after the hard winter of 2013/14 there is much work still to do. A reporter from *Golwg* magazine thought it paradoxical that I could love both urban Grangetown and rural Ceredigion. That isn't a paradox to me at all, especially as I believe that the most beautiful words in Welsh are Morgannwg and Ceredigion. It was a shame to see Tafarn y Gors following the fate of so many pubs by closing, but a joy to see it re-open under a publican who has connections with Bwlch-llan. I received a letter from the authorities asking what I did with regard to sewerage, and was able to reply by saying that I timed my 'necessities' with the opening times of the local pub. I received no further correspondence. It is delightful to spend the occasional evening in Aberystwyth, where I enjoy Dilys's welcome at Gannets, and it is pleasant to visit Llanfihangel-y-Creuddyn, where the food at the Farmers is deservedly known far and wide.

I have been many times to Brittany with Anna, Ian and the children, in the main to satisfy Anna's desire to eat oysters. Her favourite restaurant is the open-air one across the estuary from Landevennec Abbey. There you can throw the shells into the sea – the children delight in seeing the gulls swoop down to pick at the flesh that remains – and watch boats sailing in the channel. Anna's record at Landevennec is thirty-one oysters in a single sitting but she has also gained a certain notoriety at one of Cardiff Bay's restaurants by choosing oysters as her first course, her main course and her final course. The grandchildren are very fond of going to Brittany, and it was a matter of considerable pride to Mabon when he went with his father and me to the remarkable island of Enez Eusa. Someone asked him if he had ever been to England.

'Many times,' he replied. 'It's a piece of land you have to cross in order to reach the boat that goes to Brittany.'

Janet and I try to be away at Christmas – I loathe Christmas, especially its fake Christianity, and it is a pleasure always to welcome January. We have spent delightful times in Florence, Venice, Rome, Nice, Clermont-Ferrand, Seville and Vence. (The Mas de Vence hotel is particularly charming.) In the summer of 2014 we went to Scotland with the aim of helping the campaign for independence. To begin with, I wasn't enthusiastic about Alex Salmond's plans and hopes, especially if Wales was not to gain similar benefits, but after hearing the comments of London politicians and BBC commentators, I felt that there was substance to their hopes. If I were a Scot, I would feel that my nation had been totally deceived by the British (or, perhaps, the English) establishment.

I have spent a good deal of time travelling around the country giving lectures and I have done so in every town in Wales and in a number of villages. It was a special honour to be asked to speak at the celebration of LGBT month, especially in the Senedd. It was strange and splendid, after the centuries of scorn LGBT people have suffered, to be able to address members of the movement in such a distinguished setting (see www.lgbtnetwork.eu). In the meeting, there was an interesting discussion about same-sex marriages. As a test of equality, everybody was in favour but a great many hoped that the main religious denominations would not get the right to hold services for people of the same sex. As one member said, 'Considering the way people like us have been treated by the main religious denominations over the centuries, it would be servile to get married in one of their places of worship.'

I enjoyed myself making programmes for the series *History Hunters* and I took part in many discussion programmes. The one I remember best of all took place in the heart of Montgomeryshire, where the locals were fanatically opposed to wind farms. I asked whether they or their parents had ever burned coal. Everyone there agreed that they had. 'You got your heat from places like the Rhondda,' I said. 'Now it's your turn to make a contribution.' Nobody in the audience was willing to applaud such a remark. I had more pleasure describing the places in my book, *Wales: 100 Places to See Before You Die*. When I reached seventy-five, my old friend Dyfrig Davies arranged to make a programme about my life, and it was lovely to wander around Grangetown, visit the Rhondda, and be filmed at Y Gors. It was making that programme, together with my son-in-law's comment that I languished when I wasn't writing, that led me to embark on this volume. I was in Malaga when Dyfrig's programme was broadcast and, as I am convinced that seeing oneself on television is an unpleasant experience, I do not intend to watch it. However, the Welsh speakers of Grangetown are delighted that the place has been put on the map, and Dyfrig tells me the programme was well received. My sister, who can receive S4C programmes in Sussex, was of the opinion it made me look eccentric; Janet's response was, 'Maybe that was his intention.'

Now that I am seventy-six, I have started to muse about how long I am likely to live. It may be unwise to start writing an autobiography; it will be impossible to finish it, because when the end comes it is unlikely that I will be able to compose the final sentences. I read somewhere that it is possible to predict the date of your demise by dividing the difference between the ages of your parents when they died and adding five years to take account of medical advances. Medical friends tell me that this formula is nonsense, but this is the result in my case: I should die in October 2021, a date that gives me another seven years.

If I am granted my health, I have plenty left to do. In seven years my eldest grandchild will an adult, and it will be a pleasure to see all six of them growing up. I have a wealth of ideas about developing the garden at Y Gors and I would like to write at least two more books – one which will, I hope, be a Welsh version of that remarkable volume, *A Basque History of the World*, and one that will be kinder to the A470 than Ian Parri's book. I have not visited Russia, China, South America or Africa (apart from Egypt and Morocco) and I would love to return to India, so there are plenty of places left to wander in. There are places in Wales, too, that are unfamiliar to me. For example, I have only been once, and that in a hurry, to Pwllcrochan and Rhoscrowther.

If I do not have good health, the best thing I can do is to remember my mother's words: 'If you cannot do the things you want to do, it is better that you should go tidy' – even though I doubt whether I would be able to 'drain the last dregs of bitter, without nervousness on my lips' as a Welsh poem puts it. Then, of course, it will be necessary to dispose of my remains. I am an admirer of the traditions of the Zoroastrians, who believe you should not pollute water or soil or fire with the bodies of the dead. When I was in Mumbai, I went to see the Towers of Silence on which bodies are placed so that birds can eat them, and I should like to have a comparable ending. There is a place in my orchard at Y Gors where I could be placed on marble slabs and offered up as food to the red kites which are numerous in the area. That would be an excellent way of leaving this life, but no doubt there are rules against it. If it is not possible to erect a Tower of Silence at Y Gors, I shall leave all the arrangements in Ianto's care. I am certain that he will make sure that the way in which my remains are disposed of will not contain any element of Christianity.

A Life in History is just one of a whole range of publications from Y Lolfa. For a full list of books currently in print, send now for your free copy of our new full-colour catalogue. Or simply surf into our website

www.ylolfa.com

for secure on-line ordering.

Talybont Ceredigion Cymru SY24 5HE
e-mail ylolfa@ylolfa.com
website www.ylolfa.com
phone (01970) 832 304
fax 832 782